"It Is The Lord!"

John 21:7

(A cry of a heart touched by the warmth of God's grace)

By

Leandro (Lany) Maniwang Tapay
Former Diocesan Director
The Pontifical Mission Societies in the United States
Diocese of Columbus, Ohio

Lovingly dedicated to my children, grandchildren
great-grandchildren

"100% of the royalty of the book goes to the group, association, foundation
and the church that sold the books."

Noble Works Media

Contents

"It Is The Lord!" It is a compilation of
reflections on
"God moments" in the hustle and bustle of
daily living.

A ***"God moment"*** is a personal encounter
with God; it
is a moment when one may experience
God's presence,
purpose and love.

A ***"God moment"*** may present itself
through a message
from the Scriptures, or ordinary situations and
events in our daily lives.

Another way of being with God is
when we pray -
when we pray not only before eating or
before going to
sleep, but when we pray every moment.

Acknowledgments

I would like to thank….

- Patrick Andrew Crawford, my grandson, for the cover design.
- His Excellency, Patricio Buzon, SDB, DD, (my former student at Cebu Boys' Town, Cebu City, Philippines), Bishop of the Dioceses of Bacolod, Negros Occidental, Philippines for his foreword.
- Bridget Gabrielle Grim, my granddaughter and Terry Nance, a former teacher, coach and Athletic Director of the London (Ohio) City Schools for their introduction.
- Tim Puet of the Catholic Times, the Columbus diocesan newspaper – for his guidance and initial editing of the manuscript.

Foreword

Pope Benedict XVI believed that the greatest crisis facing the Church and the world today is the absence of God. Man has created a culture and a way of life devoid of any transcendent dimension or any orientation toward the sacred, thereby stripping himself of "any sure protection against the depredations of power or, more importantly, any clear understanding of the meaning and ultimate destination of his life."(Moynihan, The Spiritual Vision of Pope Benedict XVI)

God is present, of course, everywhere. He is the omnipresent power that holds everything in existence. The absence of God referred to by Pope Benedict lies in the mind and heart of man, in his lack of awareness and his indifference to God's action. We live in a world so secularized that we often experience the absence of God more than his presence. Somehow we live no differently from atheists, not because we deny God's existence, but simply because "God is absent from [our] ordinary consciousness and lives... God is not enough alive or important in [our] ordinary consciousness." (Rolheiser, The Shattered Lantern) As the English poet,Elizabeth Barrett Browning, keenly observed:

Earth's crammed with heaven,
And every common bush afire with God,
But only he who sees takes off his shoes;
The rest sit round and pluck blackberries.

It is for this reason that I commend and congratulate Lany for writing his book, "It Is The Lord." The book does not only remind us of God's presence but, more importantly, it helps us to recognize him in the ordinary happenings of our everyday life. In the book, Lany recounts the many little theophanies or manifestations of God in his own life which he calls "God moments."

He sees God in his moments of joy as well as in his moments of frustration. He felt God's compassion in Miss Racho's forgiving silence, and he heard the call to surrender himself to God when he fell victim to the malicious machinations of a new co-worker in the school.

"It is the Lord." These were the words uttered by the apostle John when he saw the resurrected Christ on the shore of Lake Tiberias after spending a long and unproductive night in the sea. Why was it that only John recognized the Lord and the other six disciples did not? I can only think of two possible reasons: John's simplicity of heart and his love for Jesus.

Jesus proclaims the pure of heart blessed because they shall see God. John was the youngest of the apostles, and hence the more innocent and perhaps the least corrupted? He is often referred to as the virgin apostle. But more than bodily continence, purity of heart here refers to the honesty of a person, his single-mindedness and lack of guile or duplicity. True, John had a hot temper and was ambitious, but he presented himself to the Lord as he was. He was flawed but simple and sincere.

The second reason why John was able to recognize the Lord was his great love for him. I believe that among the apostles John proved to be the one who loved Jesus most. When everyone abandoned Jesus during his passion, only John followed him up to the foot of the cross on Calvary.

And why such an unparalleled love? I think it is because John too felt that he was the apostle most loved by the Lord. In his gospel, he refers to himself as "the disciple whom Jesus loved" and who "leaned back close to Jesus' chest" at the Last Supper. (Jn 13: 23,25)

The great secret of the Little Prince, taught him by the fox, is that "it is only with the heart that one can see rightly; what is essential is invisible to the eye."

Pope Benedict XVI puts it more directly: "Only with the heart can we see Jesus. Only love purifies us and gives us the ability to see. Only love makes us recognize the God who is love itself."

It is no wonder then that Lany could easily recognize the Lord in the happenings of his life. Those who are close to Lany know him as a man of simplicity, a humble person who is not ashamed of his humble beginnings. At the same time, they also know him as a man endowed with an extraordinarily big heart for God and for everyone who crosses his path.

On a personal note, I wish to thank Lany for writing his book. It has helped me become more focused on my mission and better prepared for my final homecoming.

As a priest, I am aware that my primary call is to proclaim the gospel, the good news of salvation. I am also aware that what I am sent to proclaim is not so much a doctrine or a way of life, but "what [I] heard, what [I] have seen with [my] eyes, what [I] looked upon and touched with [my] hands." (1Jn 1:1) As Pope Benedict often reminded, evangelization is the proclamation of an event and an encounter with a person, Jesus Christ. My mission of proclaiming the gospel will therefore be more credible and effective when it becomes a testimony of my own experience with the risen Lord.

I am now more than seventy years old, thus living on a bonus. Doesn't scripture say that 70 years is the span of a man's life, and 80 for those who are strong? I am aware that at any time I will have to leave. I hope that when that day comes, it will not be one of fear and trepidation, but one of joy and expectation.

That is why while still on earth, I must learn to be familiar with the Lord and recognize his face, so that when he finally comes to take me to the Father's house, I shall not be afraid but excited to see him and say, "It is the Lord!"

+ Patricio A. Buzon, SDB, DD
Bishop of Bacolod
17 March 2024

Dear Reader,

Withdrawn from my previous routines, lifestyle, and social activities to focus on, caregiving I feel isolated and disconnected from everyone.

While I was wringing my hands feeling hopeless about the situation I was in, I got the inspiration to write down my thoughts and share them with those who care to read them. (Even when the time to write is illusive).

With that inspiration, the "*It Is The Lord*" came into being.

"*It Is The Lord*" came into being out of my feeling of helplessness and hopelessness.

I pray that the reflections I share in "*It Is The Lord*" will make you more aware of the "God moments" in your daily life.

Thank you for allowing me to share these reflections with you. May these reflections be a blessing to you.

Please pray for my wife and me. And please know that you, too, are in our thoughts and prayers.

May God continue to bless you and your loved ones,

Praise the Lord!

Sincerely yours in Mary of Mount Carmel,
Lany

P. S. I am on Facebook and this is my website: https://www.lanytapaywrites.com/

Other results of the wringing of my hands:

- *Fragments from the Table of Life*
- *Footprints in the Sand of Caregiving*

Prologue

Jesus often met people in the hustle and bustle of daily living.

Jesus met James and John, Peter and Andrew, while they were mending their nets at the north shore of the Lake of Galilee; Matthew, at his tax collectors' booth; the Samaritan woman, at a well fetching water; Zacchaeus, at the top of a sycamore tree.

This is one of my favorite scenes in the Gospel – Jesus standing on the shore though none of his disciples recognized Him.

"Hey guys, have you caught anything to eat?" Jesus asks them.

"Not a thing!" They answer.

"Cast your net off the starboard side and you will find something," Jesus says.

So, they make a cast and take in so many fish that they cannot haul in the net.

"It is the Lord!" John cries out to Peter.

"It is the Lord!" This is a wonderful way of expressing our joy when our heart is touched by the warmth of God's grace.

"It Is The Lord" is a reflection of our Lord meeting us in the hustle and bustle of our daily life.

May these reflections help us become more receptive to the "God moments" in our daily lives.

Preface

"*If today you hear the voice of the Lord, harden not your heart,*" says the invitatory Psalm of the Catholic Church's Office of Readings in the Liturgy of the Hours.

What it says indicates that God speaks to us more than we realize; and that God wants to communicate with us directly and often.

God communicates with us anywhere: in church, at our place of work, in our kitchen, or wherever we are. St. Ignatius of Loyola calls this truth **"*finding God in all things.*"**

An experience of gratitude, peace, and joy are some of the ways God communicates with us. And the experience of consolation, too, in times of sorrow or hardship. Saint Ignatius Loyola calls this truth, **"*God moments*"**.

God's moments are real and are occurring all around us all of the time. They are happening whether we recognize them or not. In fact, I'm convinced we miss many of them.

Ignatius found God everywhere: in the poor, in prayer, in the Mass, in his fellow Jesuits, in his work, and, most touchingly, on a balcony of the Jesuit house in Rome, where he loved to gaze up silently at the stars at night. During these times he would shed tears in wonder and adoration.

Introduction
By Bridget Grim

Some of my earliest memories of my grandfather involve visible displays of his faith. I remember the Bible studies he took me to, the worship songs he played, the altar in my grandparent's hallway, and the masses said in their backyard by visiting priests. But what I cherish most are the conversations Dedaw (the name I call my grandfather) had with my siblings and me growing up. Through these conversations and the stories he told us, I knew his relationship with Jesus was the most important thing in his life.

Each of the short chapters that follow proclaims what a divine mercy it is that God loves and saves us. Dedaw's meditations on stories from scripture and his life richly illustrate gospel truths such as forgiveness, submission, and sacrificial love. Each chapter points to Christ. "It Is the Lord!" is not only a wealth of wisdom and truth, but a heralding of God's great beauty, mercy, and love.

The last few years have been difficult for my grandfather. He has died to himself in countless ways as he cares full-time for my grandmother. Yet his hardship has not been wasted. Watching him endure various trials while continuing to love his wife and his God has been, for me, a powerful example of Hebrews chapter 12, verses 1-3:

"Therefore, since we are surrounded by so great a cloud of witnesses, let us also lay aside every weight, and sin which clings so closely, and let us run with endurance the race that is set before us, looking to Jesus, the founder and perfecter of our faith, who for the joy that was set before him endured the cross, despising the shame, and is seated at the right hand of the throne of God. Consider him who endured from sinners such hostility against himself, so that you may not grow weary or fainthearted."

The contents of "It Is the Lord!" expose a heart that has learned to endure trials by looking to Christ alone for strength and comfort. Instead of giving in to the temptation to control the circumstances of our lives, Dedaw shows another way available for believers. He reminds us of the beauty of opening your heart to God's plan and allowing God to write his story on your life. Rather than grasping for self-sovereignty and comfort, Dedaw exhorts his readers to surrender and trust in the Lord.

In "It is the Lord!", Dedaw writes that faith is not something private, but a gift to be shared. I praise the God who gifted my grandfather with such deep faith, and I pray that God would give me the same boldness and love to share my faith as Dedaw has.

"Blessed is the man who remains steadfast under trial, for when he has stood the test he will receive the crown of life, which God has promised to those who love him." -James 1:12

Introduction
By Terry Nance

I must begin this introduction by stating emphatically that I am beyond humbled that Lany asked me to do this for him.

I arrived at London High School in 1977 as a teacher and coach. For the next 33 years, I worked with Lany and considered him to be one of my most trusted and respected colleagues. For 20 years of my tenure, I was also the athletic director. Our office locations made us next-door neighbors during this time period. A vivid memory of Lany occurred on September 11, 2001. When word of a plane hitting one of the towers first hit the airwaves, Lany came into my office, and we watched that day unfold on television. The conversation was in short order as we were having a difficult time comprehending and understanding the enormity of what we were witnessing live. In my heart and mind, I know that Lany was busy praying for the victims, the first responders, and everyone touched by this horrendous event.

Lany's first book **"*Fragments From The Table Of Life*"** is a must-read. The book details his entire life with many holy scripture references that helped guide his life of reverence for and reliance on Jesus Christ. He relates the difficult times in his life as well as the blessed times. This is a man of great faith.

The second book **"*Footprints In The Sand Of Caregiving*"** describes the portion of Lany's life as the 24/7 caregiver for his ailing and beloved wife Delores Jean Tapay. This is a very difficult and heart-wrenching time for both Lany and his wife. They are not able to enjoy their retirement as planned. The emotions that are brought out in this phase of their life together are sometimes raw. Believing that Delores cannot receive adequate care in a facility, he takes this massive endeavor on his shoulders. As expected, Lany relies on his faith in the Lord to navigate the daily travails of a caregiver.

Currently, *"It Is The Lord"* speaks to his ups and downs in life and how he has managed these changes through faith with backing from the Holy scriptures. As Lany mentions, he makes "lemonade from lemons". Some of these life events could easily generate anger, resentment, and depression; however, Lany relies on and teams with the Lord to navigate these hardships.

These books are a trilogy of Lany Tapay's life and the ways he has lived that life with a solid foundation of faith through prayer and his relationship with Jesus Christ. Lany is, without question, one of the most impactful persons I have encountered in my life. I feel blessed that our paths crossed, almost daily, for 33 years. In my heart, I know that there is a reserved spot in heaven for this gentleman. I pray that he has peace and happiness in abundance for all the days he has remaining on this earth. Lany has earned all the blessings that come his way.

CHAPTER 1

To forgive is an act of reverence to God

It happened on a Friday before the opening of a new school year.

I could not believe what was happening. One minute, I was the chairman of the London (Ohio) High School guidance department; the next minute, in the middle of a department meeting, I was replaced.

"Lany, you step down. You are no longer the head of the department. I am. During the lunch break, I talked to the Superintendent and he told me to take your place." A newly hired co-worker told me when the meeting resumed after lunch.

At first, I thought the new co-worker was playing a joke on me. Unfortunately, it was not a joke.

I knew leadership positions come and go.

But my heart was broken in the manner it was done.

Neither the superintendent nor the principal informed me of my demotion.

It was so weird. It was cruel.

There was no phone call, no email, and no memo about my demotion. There was no warning.

It was done publicly. A non-administrator executed the demotion. It was done by a newly hired co-worker.

It was done while I was presiding at a countywide meeting of counselors, school nurses, and attendance officers.

My demotion was orchestrated and executed by my new co-worker, a lady of my size. Can you imagine that?

It was unbelievable. It was like a coup d'etat.

Everyone in the meeting room looked at each other with surprise and disgust as the coup unfolded in front of their very eyes.

It was an insult to my career and my personhood.

And there I was, like a timid little boy stepping down from the podium with a fake smile, while the bully stepped up to replace me in a position that I held with great pride and diligence for several years.

It reminded me of my homeland, the Philippines when Ferdinand Marcos destroyed democracy and made himself a dictator.

"This lady is a dictator!" I thought to myself. Correction: "This woman… She did not deserve to be addressed as a "lady" by the way she behaved.

I had heard stories about workplace shootings by disgruntled employees.

I was so disgruntled that were it not for my faith in God and my being gifted with a good mind, I would have shot the newly hired coworker, the principal, and the superintendent.

It is a blessing I never wanted to own a gun.

To this day, I wonder why the superintendent, the principal, and myself kowtowed to this newly hired woman.

She was a mean woman. In my book, she was the wicked witch of Madison County.

I do not know why the superintendent and the principal did not discuss my demotion with me. It is a mystery I will take to my grave.

I was hurt. I was angry. My first thoughts were of revenge and getting even.

I longed for justice. I relished the thought of vengeance.

Several options flashed through my mind while driving home to Columbus at the end of that awful day.

But thinking of my wife and children prevented me from doing something stupid and irreversible.

At one point on my way home on Interstate 70 East from London to Columbus, a scene flashed through my mind.

I had a "God moment"!

It came when I thought of the scene from Scripture of Joseph's brothers in Egypt.

Joseph's brothers did not recognize him but he recognized them, though they had larger stomachs and less hair than when they last saw him 20 years earlier.

The last time Joseph saw his brothers' faces, he was looking up from the bottom of a deep, dry well.

The last time he heard their voices, they were laughing at him.

The last time his brothers called Joseph's name, they called him every name in the book.

"Get even?" "Revenge?" These were in Joseph's power. But these were never in his mind and heart.

Joseph was in control because he had the highest position in Egypt. He took orders from no one except the Pharaoh.

With a snap of Joseph's fingers, his brothers could become deviled eggs.

Joseph could order the guards to bind their hands and feet and show them what an Egyptian dungeon was like.

But Joseph did not do any of this.

Why?

Vengeance was in Joseph's power. But he understood that the power of revenge is toxic.

I know. I have tasted it. Have you?

The fleeting pleasure of revenge is not worth it. The aftereffect is so bitter.

Rather than get even, Joseph revealed his identity to them.

Then he ordered his family to be brought to Egypt. He granted them safety and provided them with a place to live.

Vengeance belongs to God. If it belongs to God, then it is not mine.

I searched the Scripture and could not find the command "get even with those who hurt you."

No one could ever find it because God never commanded it.

Instead, God said, "Vengeance is mine. I will repay" (Hebrews 10:30).

"Do not say 'I will pay you back for the wrong you did. Wait for the Lord, He will make things right." (Proverbs 20:22).

Judgment is God's job. To assume otherwise is to assume that God can't do it. And such an assumption would be irreverent.

To forgive then, is to show reverence to God.

When I forgive you, I am saying "God is fair and He will do what is right."

When I went back to work on the Monday after my demotion, I turned a new page in my life.

I decided to follow Joseph's example. I resolved to wait for the Lord and believed that God would someday make things right.

I resolved to work with the cards in my hand.

As the teachers' union prepared to fight my demotion in court, I told them not to proceed.

The union had already contacted the union's lawyer, who was waiting for an order from me to proceed.

To add insult to injury…

"Lany, the new counselor will be in charge of the junior and senior classes. You will have freshmen and sophomores." The principal told me, peeking in my office doorway.

I did not understand why he did not enter the office, sit down, and discuss the issues civilly.

I felt something fishy was going on.

"Thank you for at least telling me," I replied in a peaceful voice.

The situation did not bother me anymore because I knew God would take care of it.

And God did.

A few years later, my co-worker resigned and told the Superintendent that I was restored to the chairman's position.

The superintendent complied and I became the head of the department again.

It was wild, do you think so?

My tenure at London High School lasted 35 years without interruption, which made me one of its longest-serving employees.

I believe that God had orchestrated a situation for me to last 35 years at London High School.

I believe that it was in His plan that the position of Directorship of the Missions Office at the Diocese of Columbus to become vacant on time I retired from London.

Praise the Lord!

CHAPTER 2

Oh my God, How Great Thou Art!

It was 1945. World War II had just ended. The Americans had liberated the Philippines.

Led by Gen. Douglas MacArthur, the American liberation forces had kicked out the Japanese invaders from the country.

Three years earlier, at the height of the conflict, Gen. MacArthur left the country for Australia, where he organized the liberation forces.

"I shall return!" the general said when he left.

The country was hanging on to MacArthur's words while waiting for the day when he would return. His words gave hope to the country.

"I shall return" sustained the Filipino and American forces who fought the Japanese during MacArthur's absence.

After the war, the American government instituted rehabilitation programs that helped rebuild the Philippines, along with programs that promoted a democratic system of government in the country.

One of the most effective means of educating the nation on democracy was through the efforts of the USIS (United States Information Service), stations that the American government established all over the country.

The service promoted democratic government through forums, books, and other means.

The USIS became very popular among Filipinos, particularly because its cinema program attracted residents of the towns and villages.

In Balilihan, my hometown, folks from all areas surrounding the town walked as far as three or four miles to the central plaza to watch the movies.

They used torches made of dried coconut leaves to lighten their path as they walked to town, for there were no electrical services in the area.

The USIS brought its big generators to generate the electricity needed to show the movie.

The USIS orchestrated the show very well.

The presentations opened with remarks by then President Harry Truman, followed by a few cartoons that were intended to help people develop good health habits and practices to prevent the spread of tuberculosis.

At the time, this disease was rampant and there were no medications for the malady.

Folks who contracted tuberculosis were sent to a sanitarium. My extended family had some members sent there.

The main attractions were cowboy movies.

In the Philippines, there are cows and horses, but no cowboys.

"I would like to be a cowboy when I grow up. How could I become one?" I thought.

I pictured myself in cowboy attire, smoking a cigarette and wearing a cowboy hat and kerchief.

I would be hard-riding and slow-talking and my best friend would be a horse.

I thought the cowboys were cool guys. They were my heroes.

My dream of becoming a cowboy changed when I played a shepherd at an elementary school Christmas play.

It was then that I learned more about shepherds. On the surface, a shepherd is similar to a cowboy.

Like a cowboy, a shepherd, too, is rugged. He sleeps where jackals howl and works where wolves prowl.

He is never off duty and always alert. Like a cowboy, he makes the stars his roof and the pasture his home.

But the similarity ends there.

The shepherd loves his sheep, while a cowboy does not love cows. A cowboy may appreciate his cows, but he doesn't know them the way a shepherd knows his sheep.

I have never seen a picture of a cowboy caressing a cow, have you?

But I have seen pictures of shepherds caring for their sheep with love and tenderness.

Why the difference?

It's simple.

The cowboy leads the cow to the slaughter. The shepherd leads the sheep to be shorn.

The cowboy wants the meat of the cow; the shepherd wants the wool of the sheep.

So, they treat the animals differently.

The cowboy wrestles, brands, herds, and ropes.

The shepherd leads, guides, feeds, and anoints.

The cowboy whoops and hollers at the cow.

The shepherd calls the sheep by name.

I am glad Jesus did not call Himself "The Good Cowboy."

No flocks ever grazed without a shepherd and no shepherd was ever off duty.

When the sheep wandered, the shepherd found them.

When the sheep fell, he carried them. When they were hurt, he healed them.

Sheep are not smart. They tend to wander into creeks for water and their wool grows heavy and they drown.

They need a shepherd to lead them to calm waters (Psalm 23:2).

They have no defense – no claws, no horns, and no fangs.

Sheep are helpless. Sheep need a shepherd with a rod and a walking stick (Psalm 23:4) to protect them.

Sheep have no sense of direction. Sheep need a shepherd to lead them on the right paths.

So, do I. I tend to be swept away by waters I should have avoided.

I have no defense from prowling lions seeking someone to devour.

I, too, get lost. I have wandered away like a sheep and have gone my way (Isaiah 53:6).

I need a shepherd. I do not need a cowboy. I need a shepherd to take care of me and to guide me.

And I have One, and He knows my name.

God knows our name. What an amazing truth.

Think about it.

In all of eternity, we were in God's mind. We were in His mind even before we came into being.

When I was a little boy, I used to go up a hill near my house on clear nights.

I laid down on the grass and gazed at the heavens and wondered how great God is, Who created the heavens and the earth.

I did not know it then, but now I know.

God created a vast universe. So vast, that some of the stars in heaven that we now see, no longer exist.

Think of it; the earth, which we call home, is only a tiny dust in the universe.

And on this earth, exist human beings created in the image of God.

And this God knows our name. When I think of it, when I think of what Christ had done for us when we had fallen from grace, my soul could not help but sing: "Oh my God, how great thou art."

And what a mystery of love and mercy it is!

This God, Who created the vast universe and Who redeems the world, is Our Father.

CHAPTER 3

A letter that changed my outlook on life

A person who is admitted to a religious order makes a vow of poverty, along with chastity and obedience.

On the surface, it appears that the vows make a person less free and more confined or restricted.

Ironically, the opposite is true. In reality, the vows make a person more free.

After I was admitted to the Salesian congregation and made the three vows, my worries about what to eat and wear and where to live ceased.

As a result of the vow of poverty, for a few years, I lived a worry-free life.

Scripture says that whatever you give to God will be returned a hundredfold (Mark 10:29-30).

This is an even more pronounced reality for a person who enters a religious order. As St. Francis of Assisi said, "It is in giving that we receive."

I left the Salesian congregation with full knowledge of the consequences of my decision.

I knew that the worry-free life I enjoyed for a few years would end.

I knew that starting a new life would be a challenge, especially since I came from a different country (the Philippines) and a different culture.

In America, I had no family to help me during the transition. The absence of a safety net made my decision to leave the congregation more scary.

Fortunately, while at Josephinum, I was recruited to work in a team that put on a Cursillo weekend retreat at Holy Cross Church in Columbus.

During that weekend, I befriended a few people in attendance. I turned to them for help when I left the Josephinum.

Looking back, I could see that it was a part of God's plan for my life, for God used *cursillistas* in my transition from the religious life to that of a layperson.

A *cursillista,* who was the chief financial officer at the St. Therese Shrine Center at the time, loaned me some money interest-free to help me start a new life in America.

To supplement the cash I borrowed, I wrote a letter to a few *cursillistas* to beg for help while I was looking for a good-paying job.

But I dropped my begging activity like a hot potato after receiving a three-page letter in response.

"Stop begging! Go to work! You are not in the Philippines." The letter said.

I could not believe what I read. I thought it was a big joke, but it was not.

As I read the letter, it felt as if I was hit in the face by a bunch of 2-by-4s.

I was shocked. I was angry. I felt humiliated. I felt belittled. With my blood boiling, I tore the letter up and threw the pieces in a trash can.

Then I had a moment of "It is the Lord."

After I recovered from the initial shock, a thought flashed through my mind.

"I am a healthy person. I should not beg. I should support myself." I told myself.

Looking back, that was the best letter I ever received after I left the congregation.

It changed my mindset from relying on others to self-reliance. The letter was God-sent; it was a blessing in disguise.

Though it was hard to swallow, it gave me a better understanding of the American culture of "self-reliance" and the "do it yourself" mentality.

"In America, we believe in self-reliance. If you want to live in America, you have to change your mindset, so stop begging and get yourself a job like everyone else," the letter said.

The author of the letter was right.

In the Philippines, begging is a common practice. I can still remember that during and after World War II, as children, we followed American GIs and begged for chocolate. "Chocolate, Joe," we cried.

The Philippine government also begged the American government for financial aid to help rebuild the country from the devastation caused by destructive bombings – first by the Japanese invaders and later by the American liberation forces led by Gen. Douglas MacArthur.

"Change your mindset!" the letter emphasized. And change I did.

As the saying goes, "If you give fish to a man, he has fish for a day. But if you teach a man to fish, he will have fish for life."

I embraced the "self-reliance" philosophy, even in my walk with God. I started to believe in "do it yourself Christianity, believing I had the power I needed.

Self-reliance teaches that all I had to do was to look deeper and longer within myself, and there would be nothing I could not do.

I started to believe that "God helps those who help themselves" or "God has started it and now you must finish it" or "God has done His part and now I must do mine."

I later discovered that self-reliance does not work in my walk with God.

Why?

Self-reliance does not work because the concept is framed on a faulty premise: God will work for me as long as I work; ,or my faith is strong as long as I am strong; ,or my position is secure as long as I am secure; ,or my life is good as long as I am good.

Here is the problem: My faith is not always strong, my position is not always secure and I am not always good. "No one is good," Scripture says (Matthew 19:17).

In spiritual life, the 50-50 proposition is too little. I need more than "to try a little bit harder." I need help from outside of me.

I need the kind of help that Jesus promises: "I will ask the Father, and He will give you another Helper to be with you forever – the Spirit of truth. The world cannot accept Him because it does not see Him or know Him. But you know Him because He lives in you" (John 14:16-17).

What a wonderful promise from our Father. God is not only near us, God is not only above us, God is not only around us – God lives in each one of us.

God dwells in our hearts. In the hidden recesses of our being dwells not an angel, not a genie, not a philosophy – but the God of the universe! Can you imagine it – God in you?

Think about it.

It was not enough for God to appear in a bush; it was not enough for God to dwell in a temple; it was not enough for God to become man and dwell among us; it was not enough for God to leave His Word and promise that He would return at the end of time.

God goes farther … God takes up residence in each of us.

Paul asks, "Do you know that your body is the temple of the Holy Spirit?" (1 Corinthians 6:19)

Perhaps you don't. Perhaps you do not think that God would go that far to bring you home.

If you don't, then think again.

CHAPTER 4

Mountains that God moves

My classmate Orlando ran after me. When he caught up, he grabbed my hand and said, "Hi, Lany, give me that book. Miss Racho (our first-grade teacher) said you cannot take it home. It could get lost."

"Oh my Lord, I am in trouble now!" I said to myself as I gave Orlando the book.

I was afraid of Miss Racho. She was a good teacher, but she was very strict. Everyone in class knew it. She was thin, but a mighty lady.

I was like a scared rabbit. I was caught red-handed smuggling a book from school.

At that time, only students from grades 3 to 6 were allowed to take books home. First- and second-graders were forbidden from doing it.

It was the last day before Christmas break. Our class was rehearsing Christmas carols in preparation for a music festival at church in the late afternoon.

At the rehearsal, Miss Racho assigned me to stand at the back of the group near a back wall because I did not have a good singing voice.

No one wanted to be near me during the rehearsal because my voice tended to disturb the harmony.

When I became aware that I was standing near a pile of books, an idea flashed into my mind.

"I am going to take a book to practice reading during the Christmas break," I thought.

My heart beat a bit faster with excitement at the thought of taking a book home.

After World War II, there was absolutely nothing to read where I lived in the Philippines.

Books, magazines, newspapers, and other periodicals did not exist.

When I learned the alphabet, I tried to apply it by reading the words on boxes.

The first word I ever read and pronounced was "Manila," printed on a box containing cigars from Cuba.

While everybody was concentrating on the Christmas carols, I slowly and carefully grabbed a book and hid it under my shirt.

I kept it there until the festival was over.

Then, I took the book from under my shirt and started to walk home, feeling happy to have a book to read.

But I made a big mistake.

I took the book out too early when I was still near the church. Miss Racho saw this and sent Orlando to retrieve it.

The thought of facing Miss Racho when classes would resume after the Christmas break made me sick to my stomach all through the Christmas vacation.

"How could I return to school and face Miss Racho?" I thought.

"Nanay (Mom), how many days until school begins?" I asked several times while on vacation.

There were no calendars at that time. Even if there was one, I did not know how to read a calendar.

But when classes resumed, Miss Racho did not say anything to me about smuggling.

Can you imagine what a relief it was? I was on cloud nine the whole day.

I was a different child. It was the most peaceful day I had since before the vacation began.

The impending doom did not happen.

I wonder if similar feelings of relief and peace will flood our souls when we die and hear Jesus say, "Well done, my child. Enter into the kingdom which has been prepared for you."

I did not know it then, but I know now that the feeling of relief and peace when Miss Racho did not mention my smuggling was a touch of God's grace – a tiny drop from the ocean of mercy. It was an "It is the Lord" feeling.

God's judgment has never been a problem for me. But God's grace always stunned me.

God's judgment always seemed right – the burning of Sodom and Gomorrah, the killing of the Egyptians at the Red Sea, the Israelites wandering in the desert for 40 years, Ananias and Sapphira struck to death.

God's judgment seemed logical, appropriate, and easy to swallow.

But God's grace? That's another matter. Look at some examples from Scripture.

David, the adulterer and murderer, by God's grace became a man of God's heart.

Peter, who denied Christ three times, by God's grace, became the first pope.

Little Zacchaeus, a crook, by God's grace, gave away two-thirds of his wealth to the poor.

The "good thief" crucified with Jesus was hell-bound one minute; the next minute, he entered heaven with Jesus.

Story after story, prayer after prayer, surprise after surprise. It seems that God is looking for more ways to get us home than ways to keep us out.

Read the Scripture.

I challenge you to find a soul who came to God seeking grace and did not find it; find a person who came to God looking for a second chance and left with God giving that person a lecture.

You can't find it.

Instead, you will find a shepherd in search of his lamb. With his legs scratched, his feet sore and his eyes burning, he scales the cliffs and explores the caves, he cups his mouth and calls into the canyon, and the name he calls is yours!

God is a woman in search of a lost coin. No matter that he has nine others, He won't rest until he finds the tenth. He searches the house, moves furniture, pulls up the rugs, cleans off the shelves, stays up late, and gets up early. All other tasks can wait; only one matters. The coin is of great value to Him. He owns it and will not stop until He finds it. The coin He seeks is you!

God is a Father pacing the porch. His eyes are wide and his heart is heavy. He seeks his prodigal son. He searches the horizon, yearning for the familiar and recognizable figure. His concern is not his investments or his business; his concern is his child who wears his name and bears His image. He wants him home! The son is you.

It is only in the light of this passion for saving the lost that we can understand this incredible promise: "If you believe, you will get anything you ask for in prayer."

But we cannot reduce this promise to the category of a new car, a new house, or big paychecks.

The promise of grace that God assures us is far greater than earthly wealth.

God wants us to be free of yesterday's guilt, today's fears, and tomorrow's grave.

Sin, fear, and death are the mountains God moves.

God wants to set us free so we can go home.

When we get to heaven, we will be surprised at some of the folks we will see there.

And some will be surprised to see us there.

CHAPTER 5

The Secret of the Ages revealed to a five-time divorcee

"If you intentionally do not mention a sin during confession, it is a mortal sin. If you die in mortal sin, you will go directly to hell."

Sister Veronica engraved this truth in our hearts when she prepared us for our first confession and Holy Communion.

I could not fault her for what she taught us; however, I cannot remember whether she ever mentioned God's love, mercy, or forgiveness.

What she taught us was true, but it was only half-true.

If she did mention God's love, I did not pay attention to it. And I paid a heavy price for not paying attention.

Years later, when I was 16, the truth of her warning became a reality in my life.

There I was in the confessional, ashamed of telling a sin to the confessor.

I experienced such an agonizing fear of going to hell that I told God, "I wish you would have created me as an animal, for animals have no souls."

"What am I going to do?" I asked myself.

"How am I going to get out of this situation?" And I did not know the answer to my questions.

It was the most horrible night I ever had. In the morning, I went to a little park near a church run by the Irish Redemptorist Fathers. For a few minutes, I sat on a bench thinking about my impending damnation.

As the *Ave Maria* rang from the church's tower bell – it rang every 15 minutes – tears were dripping down my cheeks.

"Mother Mary, help me save my soul," I desperately pleaded to our Blessed Mother.

Then I had a "God moment". It was an "It is the Lord" warm feeling.

It was as if Mary took me by my hand to a church nearby. I knelt in front of the Blessed Sacrament and asked Jesus to help me.

As I was sobbing, I noticed a gentle, flickering light on my tear-stained pair of glasses.

When I took my glasses off, I discovered that the flickering light came from the lit candles at the statue of the Blessed Mother in the extreme right corner of the church.

Immediately, I stood up and walked to the statue, knelt, sobbed and begged the Blessed Mother to help me get out of my hell.

When I looked up at her, I saw a red button on the wall with a sign saying, "If you are in trouble, push the button!" So, I did.

Almost immediately, I heard someone saying "Son, come with me" as I felt a tap on my shoulder.

When I opened my eyes, I saw a young Redemptorist priest standing near me.

He took me to a parlor nearby.

"Son, what is bothering you?" he asked.

The question was like a key that unlocked the hell in my conscience.

With tears in my eyes, I unloaded my burden.

The missionary let me talk and talk. As I was talking, for whatever reason, the sin that I was ashamed of confessing the day before, was not shameful anymore.

When I finished unloading my burden, I asked, "May I go to confession, Father?"

"You already did!" he replied.

At that time, I did know that confession could be administered away from a confessional box.

"But before I absolve you," he said, "promise God to believe that all your sins in the past are forgiven; that there is no sin that God cannot forgive; and not to be afraid to go to confession when you sin again."

After the priest made the sign of the cross over me and pronounced the absolution, peace flooded my soul.

It was as if I had died and gone to heaven. It was as if I had encountered Jesus in the person of the priest.

Have you ever felt that you have encountered Jesus in any way, shape, or form?

What I experienced must be like what the adulterous woman experienced when she encountered Jesus at a well in Samaria.

She had been married to five men. Her life was a mess before she encountered Jesus.

On a particular day, she went to the town's well at noon.

Why noon?

Maybe because she wanted to avoid the other women, who went to the well in the morning, or in the evening to avoid the heat of the summer sun.

Walking under the hot sun was a small price to pay to escape the women's sharp tongues.

The woman expected silence and solitude. Instead, she found Jesus.

Jesus asked her for water.

She was too streetwise to think that all He wanted was water.

"Since when does a Jew like you, ask a woman like me for water?" she asked.

She wanted to know what Jesus had in mind.

She was right; Jesus wanted more than water. Jesus was interested in her heart.

They talked.

She could not remember the last time a man had spoken to her with respect.

Jesus told her about a spring of water that would quench the thirst not of the throat, but of the soul.

That intrigued her.

"Sir, give me this water so I won't get thirsty and have to keep coming here to draw water," she said.

"Go call your husband and come back," Jesus told her.

Her heart must have sunk.

Here was a man with gentleness she had never seen before.

Now, He was asking her about her husband.

Anything but that!

Maybe she considered lying or changing the subject.

Perhaps she wanted to leave, but she stayed and told him the truth.

"I have no husband," she said.

Kindness has a way of inviting honesty.

The woman must have wondered what Jesus would do next. She must have wondered if Jesus' kindness would cease when the truth was revealed.

She perhaps wondered, "Will He be angry?" "Will He leave?" "Will He think I am worthless?"

If you have the same anxieties, pay attention.

"You are right. You don't have a husband. The man you are living with now is not your husband and you've been married five times." Jesus said.

No criticism. No anger. No "what-kind-of mess-have-you-made-with your life" lecture.

No. It was not perfection that Jesus was seeking. It was honesty.

The woman was amazed.

"There is something different about you. Do you mind if I ask you something?" she said.

Then she asked a question that revealed the big hole in her soul: "Where is God? My people say He is in the mountains. Your people say He is in Jerusalem. I do not know where He is."

Can you imagine the expression on Jesus' face when He heard the question?

Of all the places to find a hungry heart – Samaria.

Of all the Samaritans searching for God – a woman.

Of all women hungry for God – a five-time divorcee.

And of all the people chosen to personally receive the secret of the ages – an outcast among outcasts, the most insignificant person in the region.

Jesus did not reveal the secret to King Herod.

He did not reveal it to the Sanhedrin.

It was not in the colonnades of the Roman court in Jerusalem that Jesus announced His identity.

No. Jesus revealed Himself as a Messiah in the shade of a well, in a rejected land to an ostracized woman.

Jesus' eyes must have danced as He whispered the secret: ***I am the Messiah!***"

CHAPTER 6

A longing for our true home

"In my Father's house there are many rooms. If it were not so, would you have told you that I am going to prepare a place for you?" (John 14:2)

Some years ago, my wife gave me a little book called *God's Promises*. It contains promises from Scripture.

I treasure the little book, for no matter the situation, God has a promise for me.

"There are many rooms in my Father's house" is one of my favorites.

Some years ago, I was diagnosed with a hemifacial spasm, a nervous system disorder in which the muscles on the left side of my face twitch involuntarily.

A medical publication mentioned that the causes of the disorder include tumors.

In my case, it was caused by a blood vessel touching a facial nerve.

The twitching could be corrected through a surgical procedure in which a tissue or Teflon is placed to prevent the nerve from touching the muscle.

My family doctor sent me to Ohio State

University for the surgery.

The surgeon had to make a hole in my skull at the bottom of my head near the left ear to access the nerve touching the muscle.

The surgeon was very personable and kind. He seemed very knowledgeable about this kind of procedure. He drew on a piece of paper and showed me the procedure he was going to perform.

He appeared eager and confident.

"There are several nerves in the area," the surgeon told me. "I have to be very careful, for damage to one of the nerves could cause you to lose your hearing or your sight." He said.

"A hole in my head?"

The thought scared the heck out of me and provoked me to politely ask, "Doctor, how many procedures of this kind have you done lately?"

"None ever. You are the first one." He said.

"But I have done more difficult surgeries than what I am going to do on you." He tried to assure me.

"Oops! I am in the wrong place," I whispered to myself.

"Who invented the procedure?" I asked.

"Dr. Peter Janetta at Presbyterian Hospital in Pittsburgh," he told me casually.

So, I went to Pittsburgh to have the procedure done there.

At Presbyterian Hospital, my roommate was an elderly professor of classical literature at the University of Pennsylvania.

He was a devout Jew and gave me all his crackers that had lard as an ingredient.

He did not believe in a life hereafter.

"I enjoyed our conversations about life and God," he told me one evening, and I responded that I did, as well.

"I almost believe in the verse 'There are many rooms in my Father's house' which you shared with me," he told me while looking straight into my eyes.

"Many rooms in my Father's house" is indeed a tender phrase.

A house implies rest, safety, and warmth. Perhaps there is a table, a chair, and a bed. A house is a place where we feel safe.

I was 14 years old when I left my house in Balilihan, Bohol, Philippines. I went to Cebu to become a houseboy to earn my high school education.

There was no high school in Balilihan.

There was one in Tagbilaran, the capital city of Bohol. But my parents could not afford to pay the tuition to send me there.

Unlike in America, high school education in the Philippines is not free.

It was a very painful experience to leave home. I was so homesick that I thought my heart would break.

I know what it is like to be in a house that is not my own.

As a houseboy, the house I lived in for two years was not my own. I did not feel at home there.

I have spent much time in dormitory rooms and had my share of sleeping in hotels.

They have beds. They have tables. They have food and they have warmth.

But they are a far cry from being at my own father's house.

Although my father died a long time ago, it is as if I could still hear his voice waking me in the morning and telling me to get ready for school. It is a fond memory of my childhood in Balilihan, Bohol, Philippines.

As my little book of promises says, "My heavenly Father is preparing a place for me" – a place with many rooms.

An ample place with space for others. There is a special place for me and I will be welcomed.

I do not always feel welcome on earth.

I often wonder if there is a place here for me.

People can make me feel unwanted.

Tragedies and hard times leave me feeling like an intruder, a stranger, an interloper in a land not my own.

I don't always feel welcome here.

Perhaps I should not feel at home on earth.

This is not my home. Not to feel at home is not a tragedy. Not to feel welcome is not a tragedy. On the contrary, it is healthy.

The language I speak is not mine, the body I have is not mine, and the world I live in is not mine.

My home is not ready yet. But when it is, Jesus will come and take me home.

"I would not tell you this if it were not true.

I will come back and take you with me so that you may be where I am," Jesus said.

While on earth, I cling to this promise of Jesus.

I cling to this promise that my home is being prepared for me, that Jesus will return for me and that I will be welcomed when I arrive.

Here on earth, God allows us to experience the foretaste of our heavenly home.

We experience it as we watch a beautiful sunrise or sunset or, we experience the joy that comes from a family get-together or the smile of a baby.

In these moments, our heart is altogether satisfied and yet strangely lacking.

It is as if we get the shadow of the thing, but not the substance.

C.S. Lewis describes it best: *"If I find in myself desires which nothing in this world can satisfy, the only logical explanation is that I was made for another world."*

Somewhere deep in our hearts is a longing and a desire for a world beyond this world, a place beyond this place, somewhere that is free from sin, suffering, sickness, and death.

I believe that these small glimpses of happiness and joy are wonderful moments that awaken our hearts for the longing of our true home to come.

Back to my surgery in Pittsburgh unfortunately, the surgery did not solve my twitching.

I went to Pittsburgh to have Dr. Janetta perform the procedure, but he delegated one of his senior students to do it.

Perhaps I would have been in a better situation had I stayed with OSU Hospital in Columbus.

But had I done that, I would not have met the elderly Jewish professor there, whose acquaintance I truly enjoyed.

A divine orchestration, I suppose.

CHAPTER 7

The underdogs are special to God

"Now you are in big trouble, little boy! The pastor is going to get you!" The bully loudly and sternly said to me.

It was as if the bully threw a grenade and exploded it in my face.

The bully waved his forefinger at my face as he pronounced my impending doom.

"Do you realize that you have committed a big crime?" He asked me as five other older boys rushed to the crime scene.

They were like the folks in Scripture with stones in their hands, waiting for Jesus to order them to strike the woman caught in the act of adultery.

Picture the scene. Here I was, an innocent little boy who could hardly kill an ant, who was alone, harmless, and defenseless being verbally attacked by mean, cold-blooded boys who enjoyed making a little boy cry.

They broke my heart; they wanted my tears.

It happened during the summer vacation after my first-grade year at Balilihan Central Elementary School in my hometown in the Philippines.

I was attending catechism classes at the parish church.

All children of the parish reported to the catechism classes at the parish during the summer break.

I do not know why they call May and June "Summer break" when unlike in America, there are no seasons in the Philippines. Regions near the equator do not have seasons.

In the Philippines, it is an eternal summer.

During the whole year, the sun rises at 6:24 in the morning and sets at 5:56 in the evening.

Once the sun rises, the world becomes bright immediately.

And once the sun sets, the world becomes pitch-black immediately.

Twilights are non-existent in regions near the equator.

You could not see any shadow at high noon as the sun is exactly on the top of the earth.

It was late in October when I came to the United States from the Philippines.

Before entering Josephinum, I stayed at a Salesian house in San Francisco, California.

I arrived there at noon. As the Superior escorted me to my room, he told me that supper was at 7:00 P.M.

I spent the afternoon in my room writing letters to my folks and friends in the Philippines.

Letter writing was the main medium of communication at that time.

There were no cell phones, computers, or emails in those days.

I was waiting to get dark to go to the community dining room to have supper.

But it never got dark.

I discovered later that in America during Autumn the sun is still on the horizon at 9 PM.

I missed my supper that evening.

Back to my catechism classes: On the first day, I made a big mistake which I heavily paid for during the whole summer.

I mingled with the kids older than myself. It was fifth-and sixth-graders who ganged up on me.

They tortured me.

The ordeal started when I followed the bigger, older boys to a room in the choir loft of the church, where many statues, holy pictures, and an old organ were stored.

As we were horsing around at the loft, an older boy removed an enamel cover from one of the organ's keyboards and challenged me to do the same.

Gullible me. I took the bait, caused damage to the organ, which was the pastor's property and got blamed for it.

It was as if the mouth of hell had opened and swallowed me alive.

Because of what I did, my summer was a nightmare. Those rascals made me cry every day during that summer break.

Have you ever been bullied?

If you have been, then you know what I mean.

Or, have you ever bullied someone, or have you participated in bullying someone?

If you had, then you need to repent.

Fortunately, by God's grace, I believe I overcame the damaging effects of the painful experience.

And I believe that God used my painful experience to help children who were victims of bullies.

In my 35 years as a school counselor, I became a strong advocate for the underdogs.

The underdogs – "a lost ball" or, "a day late and a dollar short" or, "a small guy in a tall world" or, "one brick short of a load" or, "not the sharpest knife in the kitchen".

You pick the phrase, the result is the same.

A broken heart! A bruised ego!

If you are told these things many times, you begin to believe them. You begin to believe that you are a loser.

Fortunately, you would never hear any of this phrase from the mouth of our God.

The underdogs are special to God; they are close to His heart.

Jesus touched the festered skin of the leper; He cupped his hands on the face of a prostitute; He responded to the touch of a woman with a hemorrhage; He put His arm around short-statured Zacchaeus.

Over and over, God wants us to get the message that underdogs are special to Him.

What society puts out, God puts in; what the world writes off, God picks up.

To underline God's point, while on His way to Jerusalem, Jesus told a story about some workers which was a story of God's grace.

The story goes: A certain landowner went to an employment agency, he needed workers.

At 6 AM, he picked a crew; they agreed on a wage and he put them to work.

At 9 AM, he was back at the agency and picked a few more workers; they agreed on a wage and he put them to work.

At noon and 3 PM, he did the same. At 5 p.m. – you guessed it, he was back again and picked up more workers.

At the end of the day, he paid them all the same amount" (Matthew 20:1-16).

The workers were paid in the reverse order. The last hired were paid first. The first hired were paid last.

The 12-hour laborers were angry when the guys who were hired later got the same wage.

Now let's look at the story from a different angle – the choosing.

Look at the sequence of the picking. It happened at 6 AM and 9 AM, noon, and 3 PM and 5 PM.

The best workers probably were picked at 6 AM.

The not-so-good ones at 9:00 AM.

The mediocre ones are at noon and 3 PM, and the last string is at 5 PM.

Can you imagine what kind of workers were left at 5: 00 PM? The rejects, of course.

All day long, the 5:00 PM workers passed by.

They were unskilled, untrained, and uneducated.

They were hanging with one hand on the bottom of the ladder.

They were absolutely dependent upon the merciful boss giving them a chance they did not deserve.

We are the 5 PM workers.

"Consider your calling, brothers." St. Paul says. "Not many of you were wise under human standards, not many were powerful, not many were of noble birth". Paul says.

"Rather, God chose the foolish of the world to shame the wise; God chose the weak of the world to shame the strong; God chose the lowly and despised of the world, those who account for nothing, to reduce to nothing those who are something, so that no human being might boast before God". Scripture says.

Look at who God chose as Apostles to change the world.

He did not choose the rich and famous.

He chose fishermen.

CHAPTER 8

It's our heart that God wants

When I was writing this chapter, Ryan, my grandson, was spending a week of Easter vacation in my birth island province of Bohol, the Philippines.

Ryan is working at Subic Bay, which used to be the largest overseas military installation in the United States.

After its closure in 1992, the Philippine government transformed Subic into a free port zone.

Ryan is teaching English in an international school there.

The pictures that Ryan took and shared with me brought back memories of my childhood, especially pictures of the house where I was born; Our Lady of Mount Carmel Church, where I was baptized; and the Balilihan Central Elementary School, where I took the first steps on my journey to pursue higher education.

When I was growing up, there was no electricity in Balilihan, my hometown.

It was a different world. It was a peaceful world; no loud music or boom boxes.

On warm nights, I often used to lay on the grass on a hill near our house, gazing at the starry heavens and thinking of how great God is in creating a vast universe.

The world has changed so fast in my lifetime. With modern tools and devices, life seems to move faster. The world seems brighter and more noisy.

We feel lost when we are away from a phone and a computer.

At first, I was afraid of computers.

To me, a computer was like a monster.

I did not want to touch a computer for fear it might explode in my face.

But then I realized that I would be left behind if I did not learn to use computers.

So now here I am in front of my computer, hitting keys and watching the screen.

One of the things I do not like is that a computer does what I say, and not what I mean.

For example: I mean to hit the "Control" key but hit the "Caps Lock" key instead.

And all of a sudden, everything on the screen is capitalized, even though that was not what I meant.

On a few occasions, I paid a price for hitting the wrong key.

I wanted to correct one letter but inadvertently, I hit the wrong key and deleted the whole document that I had worked on for several hours.

I should not be hard on what my computer can do. After all, a computer is only a tool.

It cannot read my mind. It cannot know what is in my heart.

But considering how much I paid for my computer, I think that at least it should keep me from making mistakes over and over again.

The computer does not think.

It computes; it does not question; it does not smile.

A computer plays exactly by the rules; you push a key, and you get a response.

If you know the right key, you will get your printout.

Ignore the right key and you will need a couple of Tylenol tablets.

A computer is a heartless creature.

You cannot expect compassion from it.

Maybe that is why its operating system is called a hard drive.

I wonder why manufacturers call a computer "personal."

There is nothing personal about a computer. It is cold; it is detached. It couldn't care less about my happiness.

If a computer is different from what it is, it would not be a computer. It would be a friend.

A friend gives you what you need, instead of what you ask.

A friend knows you more than you know yourself.

Unlike a computer, a friend does not have to be turned on during the day and turned off during the night.

Some people equate a computer to a religion.

The Father is a desktop, the Scripture is the service manual and Jesus is the 1-800 number.

In this kind of understanding of God, if you hit the right key, enter the right data, and use the right code, then bingo!

You have your printout, you have your salvation.

But if you hit the wrong key, if there is a power outage, you are in big trouble.

God does not like computerized, legalistic religion.

That was why Jesus was angry with the Pharisees.

Six times Jesus calls them "hypocrites"; five times He calls them "blind.". He called them "white sepulchers" and "snakes.". Sharp words, aren't they?

Jesus was not angry with the disciples over their sinfulness.

Jesus was not angry with Peter for denying Him not once, but three times.

Jesus was not angry with the Roman soldiers who whipped Him nearly to death.

Jesus was not angry with Pilate's questions.

But Jesus was angry at the Pharisees' self-righteous and arrogant attitude.

Do you remember the story of a Pharisee who once prayed in the temple?

He knelt near the altar, saying "Lord, thank you that I am a good person. Thank you that I am not like the bad guys at the back of the temple."

It could be that the Pharisee really was a good person.

It could be that he really was not like the sinners in the back of the temple.

But it was his legalistic or computerized mentality that Jesus did not like.

The Pharisees read the manual carefully, hit the right key, entered the right data, and used the right code.

But it was his heart that God wanted. A relationship with Him is what God wants from the Pharisees and each of us.

God was not happy with the Pharisees.

Why?

Because God is not a computer. God is a friend and a Father.

God is not angry at our weakness.

God is not angry at our sinfulness.

Unlike a computer, God is really interested in our happiness.

Unlike a computer, God truly loves us. God loves us even if we hit the wrong key or enter the wrong data using the wrong code.

Remember this – God loves you.

God does not love you more when you are being good or love you less when you are not being good.

God loves you unconditionally.

You do not have to work to earn God's love.

Do not worry too much about hitting the wrong key.

Just keep your heart wide open for God to enter.

CHAPTER 9

Go and sin no more, is our commission from God

One beautiful, sunny afternoon on a spring day, I was driving a newly purchased white Camaro with a sunroof.

I do not think Chevrolet makes this model anymore.

While on Schrock Road near Westerville, I went through a yellow light, which became red before I completed the crossing.

Instinctively, I looked back at my rear-view mirror.

A Westerville police officer was behind me. He did not go through the red light. He waited until it became green.

For a while, I thought he lost me, but he eventually caught up with me.

He turned on his flashing light.

I stopped and when I rolled my window down, he politely asked, "Do you know why I am stopping you?"

"Yes, sir. I went through a yellow light," I politely replied.

"It was not yellow to me," he retorted.

He took my driver's license, went to his car, and did not come back to my car for quite a long time.

I was anticipating a traffic ticket.

But when he finally came back to my car, he said, "Young man, your license is immaculately clean. I do not want to be the first one to dirty it. You can go, and be careful driving."

Wow! What a relief! I did not get what I expected. The police officer gave me a pass. It was a wonderful feeling.

Have you ever been given a pass for wicked or naughty things you have done? If you have, you know the feeling.

I felt like saying: "It is the Lord!" It was a God moment, according to St. Ignatius.

Imagine how the woman who was caught in the act of adultery felt when Jesus told her, "Neither do I condemn you. Go and sin no more."

She was on her way to death by stoning, but Jesus gave her a pass to start a new life.

According to the law, the crime of adultery carried the penalty of death by stoning.

The accusers already had stones in their hands. They were eager to execute the punishment.

The accusers, who were mostly church leaders, did not bring the woman to Jesus for permission to stone her.

They did not need it.

To their question, "Teacher, what shall we do with this woman?" They anticipated that Jesus would have two possible answers: "Go ahead and stone her" or "Give her a pass and let her go."

The accusers' question was a trap. They wanted to trap Jesus.

The accusers thought that if Jesus told them to stone her, they could accuse Him of not practicing His teachings about love and compassion.

If Jesus told them to let the woman go, they would tell Jesus that He was breaking the law of Moses.

The accusers thought that they had Jesus cornered.

The woman looked at the faces of her accusers. She was searching for compassion from them.

But she found none.

What she saw instead were their squinty eyes, their tight lips, their gritted teeth, and their hateful stares.

What the woman did not see was their stony hearts.

What she saw in their hands were rocks of self-righteousness.

The accusers squeezed their rocks so tightly that their fingertips became white.

They squeezed the stones as if they were Jesus' throat. They hated Jesus.

In her despair, the woman looked at Jesus.

She saw that Jesus' eyes did not glare with hatred.

Through Jesus' eyes, she felt as if He was telling her not to worry; that everything would be OK.

In the eyes of Jesus, she saw true kindness for the first time in her life.

Jesus looked at the woman as God originally made her.

He looked at her as if God had knitted her together.

"Knitted together" – this is how the psalmist described the process of God making humankind (Psalm 139:13).

God has created every one of us with beauty and goodness.

But we are blemished and scarred by our hatred for one another.

The woman was like a torn rug – torn by her guilt and by the anger of her accusers.

So, with tenderness, Jesus began to untie the knots and repair the holes in her life.

Jesus began by diverting the accusers' attention from the woman.

He drew something on the ground.

Every eye looked down.

The woman felt relief as the eyes of the accusers looked away from her.

The accusers were persistent: "Teacher, what do you want us to do with her?"

Jesus could have asked the accusers why they did not bring with them the man who was her partner in crime.

He too, was guilty according to the law.

But Jesus did not ask.

Instead, Jesus raised His head and invited the accusers.

"If you have never made any mistakes, then you have the right to stone the woman."

Then He looked down and drew something on the ground again.

When the accusers heard what Jesus said, no one spoke.

Feet shuffled. Eyes dropped. Rocks fell to the ground.

And the accusers walked away one by one, starting with the oldest one and ending with the youngest.

The accusers came as one but walked away one by one.

Jesus told the woman to look up and asked her, "Is there anyone condemning you?" Jesus smiled as the woman raised her head.

She saw no one. Only stones like tombstones on a burial ground mark man's arrogance.

"Is there anyone who condemns you?" Jesus asked her.

What was the woman thinking when she heard Jesus' question?

Was she thinking that Jesus was going to scold her or give her a sermon and let her go her way?

We do not know.

But of this we are sure: She got a pass from Jesus.

She did not get what she anticipated.

She was given a promise and a commission.

The promise: "Neither do I condemn you."

The commission: "Go and sin no more."

"Go and sin no more," says Jesus to us every time we repent of our sins.

Jesus is not speaking about sinless perfection.

Jesus warns us not to return to a sinful lifestyle.

When we turn to Christ and receive His forgiveness, we experience a change of heart.

Forgiveness does not excuse our sin.

Forgiveness is an invitation to walk in God's path; it is to move toward God.

We cannot experience the transforming power of forgiveness without being forever changed.

When we meet Jesus, sin no longer holds its fatal attraction.

Grace changes things. When we are born again, the Holy Spirit breaks the power that sin once had over us.

Before encountering Jesus, we may live only to please ourselves.

But when we have been forgiven, our motivation changes. We now live to please God.

CHAPTER 10

The angry God of Victorias

If you Google it, you will see the picture of a painting of "The Angry God of Victorias" in the church in the town of Victorias in Negros Occidental, the Philippines.

The scary portrayal of God was painted in the late 1950's by Alfonso Ossorio, a son of the owner of the largest sugar plantation in the world at that time.

After seeing the painting, the late Bishop Manuel Yap, the Ordinary of the Diocese of Bacolod at that time, vowed never to enter the church again.

The angry God of Victorias scared the good bishop.

The painting covers the whole front wall of the church behind the main altar.

It is a figure of a giant human being with a beard.

It is in the center of the wall, with one arm stretched to the end of one side of the wall and the other arm to the end of the opposite side.

The eyes – oh, the eyes, are so mean-looking, so mean that you would like to run away from it or it could cause you to have a nightmare.

The stern look could scare the heck out of you. It scared Bishop Yap.

The painting is Alfonso Ossorios' concept of God – an angry and scary God.

I wish I could sit down with Alfonso over a cup of coffee at McDonald's and share with him my concept of God – the God Jesus revealed to us.

I would like to share with Mr. Osorio a God whom Jesus revealed to us.

A God Who is a Father.

I would tell Alfonso the parables Jesus told, especially the parable of the Prodigal Son. (Luke 15: 11-32).

As the parable goes, there was a Jewish man who had two grown sons.

"Dad, give me my inheritance now." The younger son demanded one day.

At first, it sounded like a joke.

But it was not.

The younger son meant what he said.

At that time, everyone knew an inheritance was distributed only after the person who was giving it was dead.

Asking his Dad for his inheritance while he was alive was equivalent to saying: "Dad, I wish you were dead!" It was a first-degree insult to the father.

"Hell, no! No way, Jose!" That would have been the normal and the correct response to the son's insulting demand.

But the father did not go that route.

According to the parable, the man complied with his son's ugly demands.

With a broken heart, the man divided his property; half went to the younger brother and the older brother got the other half, which was fair.

We hear of many families that are broken because of an unfair distribution of inheritance.

The younger brother, after selling his share of his inheritance, left his Jewish home and joined a non-Jewish community.

The son's move broke the father's heart even more.

A Jew opting out of a Jewish community was considered a betrayal to the Jewish community.

In so doing, one becomes a traitor to his Jewish heritage.

The younger brother was enjoying his new and lavish life in a faraway land.

He was enjoying the proceeds of the inheritance.

While living a lavish life, he never thought of home. He never thought of his Dad and his brother.

But something happened in the land where he was living.

A severe famine occurred. As time went by, the proceeds of his inheritance were dwindling.

And dwindling fast.

His lavish living was deteriorating fast, and he eventually became broke.

He searched and searched for a well-paying job.

But he could not find one.

His situation was getting worse and worse.

Then he hit bottom.

The only job he could find was to feed pigs and clean the pigs' habitat.

He had nothing to eat.

He was so hungry that he had to eat the food for the pigs.

Can you imagine it?

A former rich Jewish young man who used to live with his father who had servants, was now working to take care of pigs and eating food for the pigs.

In the Jewish standard, this guy's situation was pretty bad.

It was pretty desperate. He hit rock bottom.

His dire situation made him think of home and of dinner time, years ago.

It was as if he could smell the aroma of a well-prepared dinner on the table, with his Dad and brother beside him.

"Then he came to his senses." The parable says.

"I am going home to my dad's house." He told himself.

Then he gathered his dirty, tattered clothes and began his journey home.

While walking home, he thought of many ways to persuade his Dad to take him back after he insulted his Dad and squandered all his inheritance.

He knew that he did not have the right to ask his Dad to be considered as his son.

He hoped that his Dad, at least, was going to hire him as a servant.

While walking toward home, he rehearsed his speech.

"Dad, I made a big mistake. I am not worthy to be your son. Please hire me as a laborer in your household."

The young man did not know that his Dad was missing him.

He did not know that all through the years he was away, his Dad was waiting for him to come home.

When he was near home, his Dad saw him coming and ran to meet him.

The father ran – this was unusual. This was unheard of. Jewish men do not run. Only servants do.

As soon as the father saw and recognized his son on the horizon, he ran to meet him.

And he embraced him tightly. "Son, I am so happy you came home." His Dad told him.

No sermon.

No reprimand.

Just "Welcome home. I love you."

The son did not have time to deliver his prepared speech; it was not needed.

"Go prepare for a big party. Let us celebrate. My son is home," the father told his servants.

"Give him clean clothes and put on his ring." The father said.

And there was a big party to welcome him home.

What happened to the young man is what happens to us when we return to God after we sin.

That is what happens to us when we return to our senses.

No matter how far away you run away from God, your return trip to God is only one step.

It is said that even before we turn away from Him, God has already prepared a way for us to return to Him.

The God I know is not like Alfonso Ossorio's God.

The God I know is a Father.

When we call God "Father," it touches God's heart.

CHAPTER 11

The day when death died

Out of the blue, while we were watching television, my grandson asked me, "Dedaw (Grandpa), why is Good Friday good?"

My grandson's question took my thoughts back to many years ago as a child growing up in the Philippines.

I thought of my Grandma, Simeona Maniwang, who had gone home to Father many years ago.

It was as if I could see my Grandma at heaven's window smiling at me.

As a little boy, I asked my Grandma the very same question.

My Grandma Simeona and my Grandpa Enrique were very devout Catholics.

I loved spending nights with them, not only because they had good food, (compared to what was served at home) but also because I loved hearing from my Grandma stories about the saints and Bible stories.

My Grandma and Grandpa were prayerful people.

Every 6:00 AM and 6:00 PM, they prayed the Angelus in Latin; at 8:00 PM, they prayed the "De Profundis Clamavi ad Te Domine" for the souls in purgatory, and the Holy Rosary along with the Litany of Loreto in Latin at 4:00 every morning.

At an early age, I learned these prayers by heart and I have learned to put Christ as the center of gravity in my life.

The Spanish missionaries who evangelized the Philippines instructed the people to go to confession at least once a year.

From the Spanish time, it was the tradition in the Philippines for Catholics to go to confession once a year during Holy Week.

During Holy Week, all paths (no cars and no roads at that time) led to the Parish Church.

Some people walked over six miles to go to church. We lived three miles away from the church.

My parents were not churchgoers. However, they went to church and went to confession on Holy Weeks.

Back to my grandson's question: "Why is Good Friday, good when it was the most horrible Friday in history – a Friday when the Roman soldiers killed Jesus by hanging Him on a Cross?

My grandson wanted to know.

I explained to my grandson what my Grandma explained to me many years ago at her supper table one evening in Holy Week.

What the soldiers did to Jesus before nailing Him to the cross was extremely cruel.

It was inhumane. They beat Him till He almost died. They mocked Him. They spat upon Him. They crowned Him with thorns.

"What kind of people were they, who were so low and so base as to spit on and humiliate a dying man?" My Grandson asked.

The soldiers were not satisfied with the insults and cruelty they inflicted on Jesus.

They also paraded Him across town with a heavy beam on His back for all of Jerusalem to see.

It was Passover weekend, so the city was full of Jews coming from all over the region to participate in the celebrations.

Jesus fell to the ground three times before He reached the top of the hill of Calvary where they crucified Him.

For three hours, Jesus hung on the cross until finally, He died.

At that time in Jerusalem, before criminals were executed, they were paraded across the city, with placards hung on their necks.

Inscribed on the placard was the crime of which they had been convicted. This was done as a form of deterrent.

But Jesus did not have a placard on His neck, though.

Had He worn a placard, your sins, and my sins would have been inscribed on it.

Why?

Because Jesus never committed any crime. Jesus was convicted of crimes you and I had committed or would commit.

Unlike all of us, Jesus never broke any of God's Commandments.

Finally, after enduring the insults, beatings, and thirst, Jesus reached the top of the hill.

Then Roman soldiers nailed His hands to the Cross.

Jesus' hands! They were innocent hands!

They were the hands that formed Adam from a mound of clay.

They were the hands that split the Red Sea.

They were the hands that summoned Lazarus from the dead.

They were the hands that touched and healed the leper.

Jesus died for our sins.

Sin entered the world when Adam took a bite of the fruit of the tree which Scripture called a "tree of good and evil."

Hanging with the Savior were all sins, from the sins of Adam to the sins of the last people who will be born before the end of time.

At the hill of Calvary, Jesus' life on earth hit bottom.

Where does everyone go when life hits bottom?

I do not know. But I know where Jesus went.

He went to the Father and prayed, *"Father, into your hands I commit my spirit."*

Jesus committed Himself to the Father.

When everything around you is imploding, where do you go? Do you go to the Father?

Do you know how deep your Christian faith is? Can we measure the depth of our faith? Yes, we can.

The depth of your faith depends on how much you believe that you are a child of God and that God is your Father.

Everything Jesus taught us can be summed up in our being adopted children of God and in the Fatherhood of God.

The prayer of Jesus, *"Father into your hands I commit my spirit,"* sustained the martyrs when they faced their death.

Peter told the suffering Christians, "Entrust your soul to the faithful Creator" (1 Peter 4:19).

The dying Stephen said, "Lord Jesus, receive my spirit" (Acts 7:59).

Toward the end of his life, Paul declared, "But I am not ashamed, for I know whom I have believed, and I am convinced that he is able to guard until that day what has been entrusted to me" (2 Timothy 1:12).

May God grant us grace to make Jesus' prayer on the cross our prayer.

May we live and die conscious of the reality that we indeed belong to the Lord, that we are children of God, and that God is our Father.

We belong to God – body and soul in life and in death.

Because Jesus died on the cross, we can – in life and in death – entrust ourselves to the Father's hands.

May we always cling to this prayer of Jesus when everything around us seems hopeless – when everything around us is imploding.

Prayer: *Father, Jesus commended His spirit into your hands. Grant us grace to follow His example to commend our life and our death into your loving hands.*

We entrust to you all we have received from you, so we shall lose nothing. You made us for yourself.

Our hearts are restless until they rest in you.

We pray in the Name of Jesus, Who gave His life for us all. Amen.

Why is "Good Friday" good? Because it was on that Friday when Jesus died. And when Jesus died, death died with Him.

CHAPTER 12

The peace Jesus gives

A registered letter from the Franklin County Municipal Court, delivered by a sheriff's deputy, finally arrived at my house and I signed to indicate that I had received it.

A month-long wait was over. It was as though a grenade had exploded in my face.

Our hope of not being sued had evaporated into thin air. I knew my family was in serious trouble.

The letter came two days before the statute of limitations took effect in a case in which a woman sued us for $100,000.00 after cars driven by her and my son, who was a minor, collided.

My son's car broadsided hers; both cars were totaled; and my son was ticketed.

My son had been covered under my insurance plan, but the plan had expired a month earlier and we didn't have enough money to pay the premium.

At that time it was legal (though unwise) to drive without insurance coverage. So, there we were – in very hot water!

"You'd better sell your house and enjoy traveling around the world." This was Doug Shaw's advice.

Doug was our lawyer and a dear friend of the family. "I have no doubt the lady is going to sue you for everything you own," he said.

Like a boat in an ocean hit by a Category 5 hurricane, my family was sinking.

My heart was deeply troubled. I prayed Jesus' prayer at Gethsemane: "Lord, please spare my family from this trouble, but if it is your will, grant us grace to go through this storm."

Deep in my heart, I believe that God always answers our prayers. I also believe that God's solution to our problems may be different from our own.

As I was reflecting on my unfortunate situation, I became more aware that Jesus never said "I will keep your heart away from trouble" or "If you follow Me, you will not have troubles."

I remember it said that as Christians, no matter how deep our faith is, we are not guaranteed a trouble-free life. I become more profoundly aware that Jesus promises to give us His peace even in the midst of troubles.

In Scripture, "peace" is mentioned 429 times.

After the resurrection, the first word Jesus uttered to the Apostles was "peace."

The Apostles were happy to see that Jesus was alive, but I am pretty sure they must have wondered what Jesus would do to them after what they had done to Him.

Instead of protecting Jesus, they all ran and hid. All of them, except John, abandoned Jesus at the time He needed them most.

So, they were waiting for the anvil to drop; they were waiting for Jesus' rebuke and scolding. But this did not happen.

Instead, Jesus said "Peace." For the Apostles, Jesus' greeting must have been the most welcome relief.

The peace that Jesus gives is not the absence of trouble. Jesus' peace does not mean no more lawsuits, no more bombs, no more conflicts, or no more suicide bombings.

Jesus' peace does not mean anything around us is calm, or our health is good, or our income is steady, or our kids are well.

Life is rarely calm. In this broken world, trouble seems to be the norm for most of us.

The peace that Jesus gives is not dependent on circumstances.

"I've told you all this so that trusting me, you will be unshakable and assured, deeply at peace. In this godless world, you will continue to experience difficulties. But take heart! I've conquered the world" (John 16:33).

Jesus' peace is not only possible; it is what we can and should expect as Christians.

There was peace in a bunker in Auschwitz in World War II where St. Maximilian Kolbe died.

It happened after an attempted escape.

Father Kolbe was a Franciscan priest. He willingly surrendered his life so another man who was a husband and father could survive.

Father Kolbe was condemned to die in a starvation bunker. But after nearly two weeks without food and water and with little air, he wasn't dead.

Not only was he not dead, but his voice joyfully singing hymns was heard by the Nazi guards and prisoners.

In the middle of Auschwitz, which was hell on earth – in the midst of conflict and trouble unlike anything most of us ever will see or could imagine – the people in Father Kolbe's bunker were singing hymns!

There was peace in that bunker. Such is the peace that only Jesus can give.

Conflict and trouble of some sort are our constant companions in this life.

For some of us, conflict or trouble is happening on a large scale – health matters, financial concerns, a broken relationship, or the death of a loved one.

For some of us, it is on a smaller scale. But whatever is going on in our lives, Jesus' words are spoken to us personally: "Peace I leave with you. … Do not let your heart be troubled. Do not be afraid."

Jesus' peace comes to us precisely in the midst of trouble.

It did to St. Paul. It did to Maximilian Kolbe. It was to a dear friend of mine who recently died of cancer.

The same Lord Who lives in them lives in you and me.

Jesus' words are not just words. Jesus wants to give us the gift of His peace.

May God grant us the grace to make our hearts always open to receive Jesus' wondrous and transforming gift – the gift of peace.

Returning to the events at the beginning of this chapter, I did not lose my house. In the same week the municipal court informed me that I had been sued, a miracle happened.

A young couple from New York moved into a house next to ours. The husband, Warren Enders, was a lawyer just hired by the Ohio Department of Insurance.

Doug Shaw, my lawyer, did not know of a recently decided landmark case in New Jersey that would significantly reduce the amount of our liability in our situation. But Warren knew.

Instead of being sued for $100,000, our liability as a result of my son's accident was negligibly small. And Warren took our case *pro bono*. Praise the Lord.

CHAPTER 13

"Come to Me," Jesus says

I accepted my friends' invitation, even though I did not know where we were going.

At that time, I was new in America. I was not yet familiar with American culture. I knew what "happy" meant; I knew what "hour" meant, but I did not know the meaning of a "happy hour."

"It must be a time and place where people do fun things that make them happy," I thought.

I did not ask any questions for fear that my friends would laugh at me again. A few weeks earlier, my American friends took me to a restaurant to have some hot dogs.

Adamantly, I told them that I didn't eat hot dogs. They told me not to worry because the restaurant served other kinds of food and I could order a hamburger there, too.

"I think the server made a mistake. I ordered a hamburger and not a beef burger," I thought.

I am glad that I did not say anything to my American friends; otherwise, they would have laughed at me again.

Little by little, I was learning English jargon. English is a difficult language to learn.

Later, I found out that hot dogs are not made of dog meat, but are sausages that go well with potato salad and a glass of cold beer.

I also found out that hamburgers are not made of pig meat, but ground beef.

I was surprised when my American friends took me to a bar for a happy hour because the phrase was new to me.

I had heard about Holy Hours and have been to many, but I never was part of a happy hour in a bar.

"Why do they call the late afternoon period in the bar 'happy hour?'" I asked myself. "Maybe because drinks are half-price."

The bar was dimly lit, the music and conversations were loud and cigarette smoke filled the place (At that time, cigarette smoking was permitted in bars).

"This is a place where people unwind at the end of a working week," my friend told me. And unwind they did.

It is true that going to a happy hour makes people forget their troubles. But more troubles come afterward. Happy hour is a temporary fix and people often pay for it with a hangover the day after.

We all crave happiness and peace in our hearts but often look for them in the wrong places. God made our hearts hunger and thirst for Him. "Our heart will not rest until it rests in God," St. Augustine reminds us.

God is like a magnet and our hearts are like pieces of iron. Whenever we seek goodness, happiness, and peace, we are seeking God, the ultimate goodness, the ultimate happiness and peace.

Jesus, the eternal Son of God, the One for whom we were created, is the only One who can lead us to true happiness and peace – a happiness and peace that lasts not only for an hour but without end.

Unlike the temporary fix of a happy hour, the happiness and peace Jesus offers are lasting and without a hangover.

Jesus knows our burdens. He knows our guilt, unconfessed sins, poor health, troubles in marriage, and frustrations over family situations.

He knows our grieving of the loss of a parent, a spouse, or a child. He knows the challenge of growing older and no longer being able to do what we once did. He knows our fears and anxieties over making career decisions.

Self-help books on finding happiness and peace are best-sellers because we all crave happiness and peace.

How can we find happiness and peace when we live in a violent, chaotic world? How can we find happiness and peace when we are living in an incredibly fast-paced world with so much noise and so many distractions, a world that tells us in so many different ways that peace is just around the corner with the next achievement, the next milestone, the next title or award?

These are all good, but unfortunately, none of these things ever bring lasting happiness and peace.

Our heart yearns for something more. Some of us turn to Eastern religions of one kind or another or to the New Age movement while looking for harmony in a chaotic world.

Unfortunately, true happiness and peace cannot come from breathing techniques or from going deeper into ourselves.

True happiness and peace can come from entering into a dialogue with a God Who has made everything that is, Who is passionately in love with us, Who has sent His Son for us to destroy the power of sin and death, Who longs to share with us not only the gift of His friendship but also the gift of His life forever in heaven.

True happiness and peace can come from personally and intimately knowing that God loves you by name, from knowing that God is offering you the grace and strength necessary to bear whatever cross you are carrying now, and from knowing that in the end, all will be well.

True happiness and peace can come from knowing God, from reading His Word, and from making time each day to talk to God. In short, true happiness and peace can come only through prayer.

We see people struggle for various reasons in many ways, simply because they are not making an effort each day to sit down and talk to God for a significant amount of time.

If we want true happiness and peace, we need to make sure we are daily in prolonged dialogue with God. We need to understand that true happiness and peace can only come from Jesus.

True happiness and peace can come into our hearts when we commit ourselves to love our neighbors and share what we have with those in need, to read the word of God daily, and to go to Mass as often as we can so we can hear the Lord speak to us. "Come to Me," Jesus says, "and I will give you rest."

CHAPTER 14

Lower the level of anger wherever you are

On happiness, the late Pope Benedict XVI wrote:

> *"When I invite you to become saints, I am asking you not to be content with second best. I am asking you not to pursue one limited goal and ignore all the others. Having money makes it possible to be generous and to do good in the world, but on its own, it is not enough to make us happy. Being highly skilled in some activity or profession is good, but it will not satisfy us unless we aim for something greater. It might make us famous, but it will not make us happy. Happiness is something we all want, but one of the great tragedies in this world is that so many people never find it, because they look for it in the wrong places. The key to it is very simple – true happiness is to be found in God. We need to have the courage to place our deepest hopes in God alone, not in money, in a career, in worldly success, or in our relationships with others, but in God. Only he can satisfy the deepest needs of our hearts"* – from a message to youth on his 2010 visit to Britain.

Happiness, a sense of contentment, a sense of well-being – we keep searching for it. We long for it. Worldwide, people profess that happiness is their most cherished goal.

At universities, courses on happiness are among the most popular.

Magazine covers everything from sexual happiness to financial contentment.

Marketing companies capitalize on people's need for happiness and contentment.

Commercials make grand promises: Do you want to be happy? Drive an Impala. Do you want to have joy? Sleep on a waterbed. Do you want to enjoy dining? Eat at the Red Brick Tavern or Brio or Molly Woo's.

Nearly every advertisement portrays an image of a joy-filled person.

Who does not want to be happy? We all do. But unfortunately, only few are.

Two out of every three people are not happy, according to a Harris poll. Smiles are in short supply.

By some estimates, clinical depression is 10 times more common now than a century ago.

Depression is the second-largest cause of disease worldwide, according to the World Health Organization.

How can this be? People are more educated. We have made advancements in everything from medicine to technology, yet many people are not happy.

What is up? How do we explain this gloom? The answer is complex.

People take many paths in search of happiness.

One path teaches "Happiness happens when you get something." You are happy when you acquire, retire, and aspire to drive a faster car, dress more fashionably,and drink more.

On this path, happiness depends on the clothes you wear, the car you drive, the trophy you hang on the wall, or the size of your bank account.

This path is all about your own happiness, peace, and satisfaction; it is about meeting all your desires. It is all about self-satisfaction, self-fulfillment, and meeting personal desires.

The other path, on the other hand, is what Jesus teaches – happiness occurs when you give.

According to many studies, if you want to be happy, do good for someone else. "It is more blessed to give than to receive" (Acts 20:35).

Why? Because giving has a boomerang effect.

Sometimes happiness seems elusive because it does not exist on its own. It is not something waiting for you to possess.

Happiness is a product of something you do. If you search for God wholeheartedly, God will find you and you will be happy.

True happiness is a by-product of your searching for God and God finding you.

This is a basic Christian teaching, yet sadly, even Christians get this wrong so often.

I once heard a television preacher say, "To find happiness, quit focusing on what's wrong with you and start focusing on what is right for you."

But that is not the way it works at all.

If we want to be happy, we should not focus on ourselves. We are to focus on God alone and seek holiness, without which no one will see God (Hebrews 12:14). Peace and happiness follow as a by-product.

This is good news. You cannot control your genetics. You are not in charge of the weather. You cannot control the results of elections. But you can increase the number of smiles in the world.

You can lower the anger level in your family, workplace, and community.

Yes, you. You can help people sleep better and laugh more.

You can hum instead of grumble. You can walk instead of stumble. You can lighten the load and brighten the road of another human being.

"If you want happiness for an hour, take a nap. If you want happiness for a day, go fishing. If you want happiness for a year, inherit a fortune. If you want happiness for a lifetime, help somebody," a Chinese proverb says.

For centuries, the greatest thinkers have suggested the same thing: Happiness is found in helping others.

"It is in giving that we receive" – St. Francis of Assisi.

"The sole meaning of life is to serve humanity" – Leo Tolstoy.

"Make a living with what you get and make a life of what you give" – Sir Winston Churchill.

"Giving back is as good for you as it is for those you are helping because giving gives you purpose. When you have a purpose-driven life, you are a happier person," Goldie Hawn said.

Jesus was accused of many things. But He was never described as a grump, a sourpuss, or a self-centered jerk.

People did not groan when He showed up. Nobody ducked for cover when He entered the room.

Jesus called people by name. He listened to their stories. He answered their questions.

Jesus visited people's sick relatives and helped their sick friends. He fished with fishermen. He ate lunch with a little guy (Zacchaeus) and spoke words of resounding affirmation. He went to weddings. He went to many parties and was criticized for hanging out with rowdy people and questionable crowds.

Thousands came to hear Jesus. Hundreds chose to follow Him. They shut down their businesses and walked away from their careers to be with Him.

"I came to give life with joy and abundance" (John 10:10) was the stated purpose of Jesus' life. Jesus was happy and He wants us to be the same.

Choose Jesus' path to happiness. We live in a lonely world. Our cities are populated with people with broken hearts.

Discouragement mummifies countless lives. The world is desperate – yes, desperate for kindness. We cannot solve every problem in society, but we can bring smiles to a few faces.

CHAPTER 15

Get drunk with God's presence

A large crowd coming from all over the Mediterranean world gathered in Jerusalem for Pentecost, a Jewish festival also known as the "Feast of Weeks."

This was a highly anticipated event in the Jewish tradition. It was the offering of the fruits of the first harvest.

This Jewish tradition was practiced in Balilihan, Bohol, my hometown in the Philippines. Families would not cook their newly harvested rice before the rice is tasted by the oldest man or oldest woman in the community. The same thing with any fruit tree.

The "Feast of Weeks" traditionally, was also an occasion for giving the law.

One morning during that celebration, there was a commotion. A loud sound of a rushing wind and a loud voice were heard.

At the same time, Jesus' Apostles who were in the crowd behaved strangely.

When some in the crowd noticed this, they shouted, "These men are drunk with new wine!"

The Apostle Peter responded, "These people are not drunk. Do you realize that it is only 9 in the morning? It is too early to see people already getting drunk, isn't it?"

Isn't it strange that when people saw the Apostles filled with the Holy Spirit, they thought the 12 men were drunk?

"The people were speaking different languages," the Scriptures say.

But is speaking a different language a sign of being drunk?

Have you, or have you heard of anyone drunk speaking a different language?

"Do not get drunk with wine," St. Paul says, "for that is debauchery; but be filled with the Holy Spirit instead" (Ephesians 5:18).

Is there perhaps a difference between being intoxicated with wine and being filled with the Holy Spirit?

Could it be that both wine and the Holy Spirit are powerful controlling agents?

What are some effects of wine on our bodies?

For one thing, it lowers our inhibitions. We say or do things when we are drunk that we generally don't say or do when we are sober.

Being drunk makes us sometimes fake friendliness and happiness. It makes us laugh easily and loudly. It lowers our body control. It leads us to stupid places and makes us do stupid things.

The Holy Spirit has the same effect on us as wine does, except the Holy Spirit leads us in the opposite direction from where wine does.

The Holy Spirit, like wine, lowers our inhibitions.

As a result, we become emboldened for Jesus. Lowered inhibitions make us bolder to do good things for Jesus and for each other. We worry less about what others think of us.

Have you been to a happy hour in a bar? It is a loud, noisy place. But I do not think it is a happy place – even during happy hours.

Joy is not something you can fake.

We experience real joy only in God's presence, where all our worries are put into proper perspective because a joyous God is there.

God's joy wells up inside you and you cannot help but laugh because your troubles seem silly.

God loves you like crazy. That is what it means to be drunk in the Holy Spirit. You find yourself in a different world – a world of God's love.

"Why do we not blow up with the energy of the Triune God which dwells in our heart?" we may ask.

We do not blow up because God's presence is not just a force or a feeling; it is a Person. It is Jesus, with His emotions and power dwelling in our weak and frail bodies.

"The Son can do nothing by Himself," Jesus said. "He can do only what He sees His Father is doing" (John 5:19).

Jesus does everything He sees that His Father in heaven does. That was why Jesus spent time praying alone with the Father.

Jesus' time with God dominated His life. Jesus did everything as a result of being connected with God.

Jesus was drunk with God's loving presence.

As a result, Jesus did things that no one else thought were possible.

Jesus waited two additional days to go to Lazarus' grave.

Jesus entered Jerusalem knowing the people were going to kill Him.

Jesus fed 5,000 people with few loaves and fish, despite the disciples' insistence to send the people away. Jesus simply saw things differently and did things differently.

It was as if Jesus was operating from a different world.

Yes, He was. He was in the Father's world.

Being drunk in the Holy Spirit is like that. When the Spirit of God is inside you in a powerful way, you have access to heavenly things as never before.

You will do things no one else thought possible. You will have access to the Father's world. You will operate out of the presence of God dwelling in your heart.

It is a humorous, exciting experience when you are laughing with joy because the Spirit of God is in you in the midst of a depressing situation.

To be drunk in the Spirit means to be filled with God's presence – with all His joy, His mystery, and His power. It is an encounter with the God of the universe.

" . . . be transformed by the renewal of your mind, that you may discern what is the will of God, what is good and pleasing and perfect." (Romans 12:2)

Living "life in the Spirit" can be described as a way of setting our hearts on the leadings of the Holy Spirit.

In his letter to the Romans, St. Paul is very clear that the power of the Holy Spirit is an integral part of the gospel that he had traveled the world proclaiming.

According to Paul, we all have some areas of our lives which are of God and very pleasing to Him, and others which are not so good.

Paul understood that only by living in the Spirit can we continue to build up those parts that are pleasing and gradually do away with the parts that are sinful and displeasing to God.

CHAPTER 16

God is the 'good pilot'

The flight from Los Angeles to Manila was a long one. It took 16 hours to cross the Pacific Ocean.

I made a big mistake when I booked my flight. I signed up for a window seat.

Stupid me, I thought I would enjoy the view while on flight.

Unfortunately, there was no view. Only dark clouds are below. From time to time, I would look down on the ocean and a flight attendant would tell me to roll down the window shade. "I can't win!" I thought to myself.

I did not know why the window shade had to be down all the time. But I did not bother to ask the flight attendant. She was not always nice.

I discovered that a window seat in a row of seven passengers is the worst seat one could have on a long flight.

Going to the bathroom was a big problem. I had to negotiate with seven big, fat passengers in my row to have access to the middle section of the plane in order to go to the bathroom.

I learned my lesson. As soon as I arrived in Manila, I changed my seat on my return flight. I signed up for a seat on the front row at the bulkhead, just behind the partition that divided the common folks and the rich and famous.

The plane took off from LA at 1:30 a.m. When the plane achieved cruising altitude, there was an announcement from the pilot's cabin: "We are getting ready for dinner."

"What? Dinner at 2 a.m.?" I asked myself. "This is crazy! Maybe the pilot meant breakfast."

I learned later that airlines flying to Asia follow Manila time.

We flew over a few thunderstorms. As we approached one, I had an embarrassing experience.

As I got out of the restroom, a loud voice came from the loudspeaker saying, "Ladies and gentlemen, this is Captain Smith. During storms, people have gotten hurt by going to the restroom instead of staying in their seats. Let us be clear about our responsibilities. My job is to get you through the storm. Your job is to do what I say. Now sit down and buckle up."

Although the announcement was addressed to the rowdy passengers stretching their legs into the center aisle of the plane, the restroom part of it fit my description.

I felt that all eyes were glued to me as I walked back to my seat.

At first, I was embarrassed and hurt. After thinking about it, though, I decided that's what good pilots do.

They do whatever it takes to get their passengers home safely.

The incident made me think of God.

God is a good pilot. He will do whatever it takes to bring me home safely.

If God saw me at risk, rather than safe, He would do whatever it takes to get my attention.

To get his attention, God moved Abraham to another land; God called Moses out of retirement; God promoted Daniel; God demoted Samson; God temporarily blinded Paul, and there are many similar incidents in Scripture.

The message of the Scriptures is to get our attention; it is God's relentless pursuit of man. God is on the hunt.

The Scriptures tell a simple story. God made man. Man rejected God. God would not give up until He won man back when Jesus was hung on the cross.

God's message is simple: "I am the pilot. You are the passenger. My job is to get you home safely. Your job is to do what I say."

God is always pursuing you. God is always hunting for you but He never forces you. God invites. God proclaims. But God never forces.

Listen closely to what Jesus is saying: "I am the bread that gives life. I am the light of the world. I am the resurrection and the life. I will come back and take you with me."

"Do you want to be well?" Jesus asked the cripple and the blind man. "Do you believe in the Son of Man?" Jesus asked Martha. And Jesus told her, "Everyone who lives and believes in Me will never die. Do you believe in this?" Jesus asked Martha.

Jesus never goes where He is not invited. But once invited, He does not stop until the job is finished. God does not stop until the choice is made, and the choice is mine.

I can hear God whisper and then shout. God will touch and tug. God will take away my burdens. God will take away my blessings. If there are a thousand steps between God and me, God will take away all but one.

God will leave the final one for me. To go to the restroom or to buckle up and remain in my seat is my choice.

God's goal is not to make me happy. God's goal is to make me His. God's goal is not to give me what I want, but to give me what I need, and if it means a jolt or two to make me go to my seat, then God jolts me. Earthly discomfort is a glad swap for heavenly peace.

Yes, my flight to the Philippines made me think of Jesus as a good pilot and me as a passenger. Jesus' job is to get me home safely; mine is to obey Him.

Back to my flight; unfortunately, I made a big mistake again on my return flight from Manila to Los Angeles.

The plane took off at 4:45 in the evening, Manila time. When the plane reached cruising altitude, dinner was served.

It was a delicious meal. I ordered lasagna, garlic bread, salad, and red wine, which was a good combination, I thought.

Toward the end of the dinner, there was an announcement on the loudspeaker, saying that drinks were on the house – or on the plane. "It is a courtesy from the flight crew members," the announcement said.

Stupid me again. I ordered Scotch on the rocks. Later, I found out the hard way that one cannot mix wine and Scotch.

And you can imagine what happened to me during the flight from Manila to LA. Thankfully, with my new seating assignment, I did not have to negotiate my way to the bathroom.

CHAPTER 17

We can't escape from God's love and mercy

Dwight L. Moody, a 19th-century preacher, was approached by a woman who needed counseling.

"These two men are always following me wherever I go," she claimed.

Moody recognized that the woman was suffering from delusion. There was no one following her.

To put the woman at ease, Moody told her, "These two men following you are David's men.

Their names are 'goodness' and 'mercy.'"

Then Moody opened the Scriptures and showed the woman Psalm 23:6: "Surely goodness and mercy shall follow me all the days of my life."

The woman was relieved. "That's wonderful! I have always wondered what their names are," she said.

What a beautiful characterization of God – a mobile God, an active God, a God tracking us, a God following us with His goodness and mercy all the days of our lives.

There is no escape from God. This is one of the greatest truths in life.

Like fugitives, we run. But ultimately, we cannot hide from God.

If we manage to dodge Him in life, we still will be exposed to Him on judgment day.

There is no place to hide from God.

Happily, though, when we give up flight and allow ourselves to be found by this relentless "hound of heaven" (as Francis Thompson describes God in a poem), we discover that God's intention is not to harm us but to bless us.

God has formed us even in our mother's womb for His purposes. God has ordained all our days before we even see the light of day.

"How precious also are your thoughts to me, oh God!" David exclaimed.

In coming to know God, we come to know ourselves.

In the blinding light of God's holiness, we recognize instantly our desperate need for inner purity.

Since we cannot escape from God, we cannot escape from the need for holiness.

When we are driving above the speed limit and pass a police car, we're likely to see flashing lights behind us with the police officer pursuing us, requiring us to pull over and giving us a speeding ticket.

In a similar way, God pursues us, but when He catches us, He does not give us a speeding ticket; rather, He showers us with goodness and mercy. What a wonderful reality, isn't it?

Why do we have the tendency to run away from God? Is it because we are afraid of Him because of our sins?

If you feel that you have run far away from God, know that the return toward Him is only one step away. All you need to do is to tell God "I am sorry." Let God with his goodness and mercy catch you.

Immediately after Adam and Eve ate the forbidden fruit and were hiding, God looked for them.

God did not wait for them to come to Him. God searched for them.

"Where are you?" God said (Genesis 3:9).

This was the beginning of God's search for man. This was the beginning of His quest to follow us with His goodness and mercy until we follow Him.

God's goodness and mercy will follow us wherever we are and wherever we go. We cannot hide from God. God will ultimately catch us.

The crew of the boat where Jonah was a passenger threw Jonah into a raging ocean during a storm.

God followed Jonah into the ocean by sending a big fish to pick him up.

The disciples battled a raging storm in the Sea of Galilee and saw Jesus walking on the waves. God followed the disciples into the storm.

Peter three times denied that he knew Jesus at Jesus' trial.

After the resurrection, Jesus had breakfast with Peter on the seashore. "Peter, do you love me?" Jesus asked him three times to redeem Peter from his three denials. God followed Peter into his failure.

A woman's heart was broken. She was a seven-time divorcee. Jesus met her at a well. God followed the woman into her pain.

Lazarus was dead for three days. Jesus arrived at Lazarus' home and brought him back to life. God followed Lazarus to death.

Ocean, storm, failure, pain, death – no matter the circumstances, God follows us with His goodness and mercy.

Do you sometimes feel that God is far away? No matter how you feel, God is always pursuing you with his goodness and mercy.

The interruptions in the rhythm of our life are God bringing us His goodness and mercy.

If sometimes our plan does not end the way we want it to, let us submit our plan to God. Let us ask God what He wants us to do.

In life, storms are inevitable. They are not a matter of if, but of when.

A storm or a trial in life is God's gift to us. God's goodness and mercy follow us in the storms and trials of our lives.

God does two things with our trials: either God delivers us from them or He shows us that we, through Him, are stronger than our trials.

These are ways God answers our prayers.

Open your heart to God and you will be surprised by God's surprises for you.

Even in sin, God's goodness and mercy follow us.

In this broken world, sin is a part of our reality. "For though the righteous man falls seven times a day, he will rise again. But the wicked stumble when calamity strikes" (Proverbs 24:16).

Whenever we sin, God's goodness and mercy follow us to forgive us, to cleanse us, and to restore us. So confess your sins. Repent and accept God's forgiveness.

Do you sometimes feel inadequate to do what God wants you to?

Know that God's goodness and mercy follow you in your inadequacy. Open your heart to God and God will give you everything you need to accomplish His plan in your life.

The realities of God's goodness and mercy are not addressed to a group; rather, they are addressed to each of us individually.

God's mercy and goodness will follow us. This is addressed to you. This is addressed to me.

There will be no day in which God's love does not follow you.

We cannot escape from God's goodness and mercy.

Surely goodness and mercy shall follow us all the days of our life.

CHAPTER 18

If you open your heart, you will hear God's voice

One of my favorite poems about God is "The Hound of Heaven," written by Francis Thompson in 1890, describing God as a hunting dog.

It's a strange portrayal of God, isn't it? But I could see the truth of the description, for a dog is known for its searching ability.

During the recent earthquake in Turkey and Syria, rescue workers used the help of dogs to search for people buried underneath the remnants of collapsed buildings.

In "The Hound of Heaven," the first stanza is my favorite because now and then, I have fled and hidden from God, as Adam and Eve did after they ate the apple.

"I fled from Him, down the nights and down the days;
I fled from Him, down the arches of the years;
I fled from Him, down the labyrinthine ways of my own mind;
And in the midst of tears, I hid from Him"

Jonah in the Scriptures is a perfect example of a man who fled from God.

Jonah was a good man. He was a prophet. He served God well. He had done many good things.

But Jonah had one big problem; He did not want to be disturbed by the way of life he had chosen. He did not want to change the status quo.

Jonah heard the voice of God telling him to preach in Nineveh and tell the people there to repent; otherwise, God was going to punish the city because of its sinfulness.

Jonah knew God. He knew that if the people in Nineveh would repent, nothing bad would happen to them.

Jonah did not want the people of Nineveh to think that he was a false prophet. "Why bother preaching? Too much hassle for nothing," Jonah said to himself. So, Jonah refused to go to Nineveh.

Instead, he went to Spain, which was in the opposite direction from Nineveh.

While on the way to Spain, the boat on which Jonah was a passenger was hit by a big storm. The boat was about to sink.

The crew suspected that a passenger who was cursed had caused the storm to rage.

At a certain point, Jonah confessed to the crew, telling them that he had done something very bad, and because of it, God was punishing him.

"Throw me into the ocean to save the boat," Jonah told the crew.

Afraid of perishing, the crew members were eager to comply and threw Jonah into the ocean.

But God followed Jonah into the ocean by sending a big fish that swallowed him and gently vomited him onto a shore. God's goodness and mercy followed Jonah, even to the ocean.

Luke the Evangelist also has a story about ways of fleeing from God (Luke 10:25-37).

As Luke's story goes, a man was on a journey. While on the road, he was robbed and beaten by bandits and left half-dead on the side of the road.

A priest traveled along the same road. He saw the wounded man but did not help him.

Why? We do not know. Perhaps he had a meeting at his synagogue and he did not want to be late.

So instead of helping his fellow man, he fled the scene and continued his journey.

A Levite was traveling on the same road and said to himself, "The man probably is going to die. I do not want to testify in court about the crime."

The Levites did not want to be involved. So, he went his own way without helping his fellow man in need.

A Samaritan also traveled on the same road. In those days, Samaritans were considered sinners.

When the Samaritan saw the wounded man, he stopped to help him.

He cleaned the man's wounds, pouring oil and wine on them. Then he put the man on his own horse and went to an inn.

He gave the innkeeper some money and told him, "Kindly take care of this wounded man. If the money I give you is not enough to cover the expenses, I will give you more when I return."

Unlike the priest and the Levite, the Samaritan spent a lot of time helping the wounded man. He lost his whole evening caring for the wounded man.

Yes, the priest arrived at his destination on time, and the next day, the Levite was happy because he did not have to testify in court.

Priests and Levites were considered good people. Both were admired and respected.

On the contrary, the Samaritans were considered sinners. But it was the sinner who took care of the wounded man.

Why did Jonah, the priest, and the Levite flee from God? It was because their hearts were not opened.

When one's heart is closed, one cannot hear the voice of God.

The Samaritan's heart was opened and because of it, he saw God in the wounded man and heard God's voice asking him to help.

Jonah had a plan for his life. But instead of allowing God to write the history of his life, he tried to write it himself. He did not want God to interfere with his plans.

The Samaritan, on the other hand, allowed God to write his history and interfere with his plans.

When God threw a wounded man before him, he responded to God's invitation to help a fellow human who desperately needed help. On that evening, the Samaritan's life was forever changed.

Do you want God to write the history of your life?

If you do, then open your heart so you can hear the voice of God. Search for God in every situation in your life. If you pay attention, you will find God in every situation – in the good and in the not-so-good ones.

If you open your heart as the Samaritan did, God will surprise you. If you open your heart, you will hear God say to you, "Go and do likewise!"

CHAPTER 19

Don't let anger control you!

There were only two checkout registers open. The lines were long. It was between 4 and 5 in the afternoon when many folks picked up grocery items on their way home from work.

After a long wait, the manager sent someone to open a third register.

I did not know why, but the customers at the end of the two existing lines were invited to go to the newly opened register.

This action of the manager angered the customers who had been in line for a while. "Why do you start checking out those at the end of the existing lines?" a man behind me barked at the manager in a very loud, angry voice.

This scared me. Not long ago, I had seen TV news reports about a shooting which killed several people at a grocery store in Buffalo, New York.

"I hope this does not escalate into a shooting incident. I hope this man is not carrying a gun," I said to myself.

"If a shooting occurs, should I wrestle to disarm the man or should I run to the closest exit?" I thought as my adrenaline started to kick in.

I probably would have run; the man was so big that he could pick me up with one hand.

It seems that nowadays, many people are walking around full of anger. They are like walking time bombs. Given the right situation, they could explode.

Have you watched the news on TV lately? Politicians are throwing verbal stones at one another and the media folks are egging them on.

It is as if news reporters are helping create an atmosphere of anger in our society.

The other day, a driver was angry at me because I w as obeying the speed limit – 45 miles per hour.

He told me to return to where I came from because I did not know how to drive in the United States. I believe his speedometer must have been registered in the 60s.

He waved one of his fingers as he passed me, making a face at me.

"He needs to participate in an anger management program," I said to myself.

Anger seems to be so prevalent in our society that courts and school systems are providing anger management programs for people who seem to have lost control of their ability to balance their emotions.

It is hard to understand why the world we live in has become so angry. Some people blame their anger on others or on situations they have encountered in their lives.

The truth is that anger is natural to a human being, just as smell is one of the senses.

I don't think that we are becoming more angry. What I think is that we are losing our ability to balance our emotions.

"Anger is an acid that can do more harm to the vessel in which it is stored than anything in which it is poured," said Mark Twain.

Anger not only wounds those it targets. It also destroys the hearts of those who nurture it. And worst, anger is contagious, like COVID-19.

Even if you feel that you are in control of your feelings, you can be sucked into the vacuum of anger if you are not careful.

You have no control over the people around you or the situations in the world that anger you. But you do have control over how you respond to them.

Giving in to anger is detrimental to us and our well-being. When we react to anger, problems are created, not solved.

If we want to be a part of the solution, we need to control our anger.

"How did Jesus handle the issue of anger?" you might ask. This is how: He said, "Father, forgive them, for they do not know what they are doing" (Luke 23:34).

This is how Jesus responded to those who tortured and killed Him. He forgave them.

Have you ever wondered how Jesus kept his cool? The answer is found in the statement "They do not know what they are doing."

Jesus did not see those who killed Him as murderers; rather, He saw them as victims. It was as though He considered those who killed Him, as He put it, "sheep without a shepherd."

If you think about it, Jesus was right. They really did not know what they were doing. They did not have the tiniest clue.

They were angry at something they could not see and they took it out on God, of all people, but they did not know they were killing God.

For the most part, it is the same with us. Though we hate to admit it, we too are like sheep without a shepherd.

When we think about it, we do not know about the realities of life. We do not know about death and eternity.

We do not know about love and hatred. We do not know about death and pain. We do not know about the aging process or how to heal all diseases. We do not know how to get along with others.

We do not know how to stop wars. We do not know how to abolish hunger. When St. Paul says "I do not know what I am doing" (Romans 7:15), he speaks for all of us. Paul is right. We do not know what we are doing.

Can you see Luke's and Paul's points? Uncontrolled anger does not improve the world.

But sympathetic understanding will make the world a better place. When we see ourselves as we are – broken – we can help.

When we see our brokenness, we begin to operate from a posture of compassion and concern.

When we see our brokenness, we can see that the lights are out and people are stumbling in the darkness, so we light candles.

"We criticize by creating," said Michelangelo. That's what the Catholic Church does – helping the poor, building schools, hospitals, and orphanages, and encouraging people to put away their guns.

There is something about understanding our broken world that makes us want to save it or even die for it.

We can't solve all the problems of the world, but we can lower the temperature of anger in ourselves and in the people around us; we can extend a deed of kindness to people around us wherever we find ourselves.

"I tell you that anyone who is angry with his brother will be subject to judgment. Therefore, if you are offering your gift at the altar and they remember that your brother has something against you, leave your gift there in front of the altar. First, go and be reconciled to your brother; then come and offer your gift. Settle matters quickly with your adversary" (Matthew 5:22-25).

CHAPTER 20

I'm always stunned at God's mercy

It scared the heck out of my friend and I. We were maybe 7 or 8 years old at that time. We were curious little boys.

As we were exploring around the choir loft of our church, we thought we had found a dead man.

Out of fear, we ran away as fast as we could. Our hearts were beating faster than our feet.

After a little while, when the adrenaline returned to normal, we hesitatingly went back to investigate what we saw.

It was then that we discovered that it was not a dead man that we saw. It was a life-size crucifix protected by a linen cloth.

At first, I was afraid to look at it. But after a while, my fear subsided. After a good look at Jesus' face, I was no longer afraid.

I was intrigued with His face, especially His eyes. They were half-opened, gazing a bit heavenward.

Jesus on the cross looked so pitiful.

I also was intrigued by the sign above Jesus' head. It read "INRI." I wondered what it meant.

I asked my mom and dad when I went home. But they did not know.

I asked my grandma and grandpa. They did not know.

Later, I learned what it meant: "IESUS NAZARENUS REX IODEORUM" in Latin, which means "Jesus the Nazarene King of the Jews."

I also learned that Pontius Pilate ordered out there as a deterrent; Pilate wanted the Jews to know that if anyone claimed to be a king, he too would be crucified as Jesus was.

The Jewish leaders did not like the sign. They asked Pilate to change it to say: "Jesus the Nazarene claimed to be king of the Jews."

But Pilate refused to change the sign. "What is written is written!" he told the Jewish leaders.

The words were written in Latin, Hebrew, and Greek.

Latin was the language of Rome. At that time, Rome was known for its form of government and controlled the area where Jesus was crucified.

Greek was the language of Greece. At the time, Greece was known for its culture.

Hebrew was the language of the Jewish people, who were known for their religion.

The sign indicates that Jesus is the king of all aspects of civilization – of government, culture, and religion.

God uses anyone or anything to carry out His plans and purposes.

As we can see, in this case, God used Pilate to evangelize.

Pilate did not know it. God used Pilate to convert a criminal.

When Jesus was crucified, two criminals were crucified near Him, one on his left and one on his right. At first, both criminals cursed Jesus. Later, one of the criminals became a penitent and the other remained cynical.

Let us talk about the penitent criminal.

By the world's standards, his life was a failure.

He made wrong decisions. He was associated with people of questionable character.

He committed one crime after another. Now he was in the final stage of his failed life.

He had reached the bottom. He had received the death penalty (Luke 23:34-43).

Watching Jesus on the cross, as he saw the sign above Jesus' head, he began to wonder who this Jesus was.

It seemed strange to him that Jesus was not angry, though He was mocked, beaten, crowned with thorns, and spat upon.

He did not see any sign of anger in Jesus's eyes, only tears.

Then he began to wonder how Jesus could be so calm in spite of all the cruelties He endured.

And then he heard Jesus say in a soft voice, ***"Father, forgive them. ..."***

Then he wondered why anyone wanted Jesus dead.

For a brief moment, his curiosity made him forget the pain in his own body and the nails on his own hands.

Then he began to feel a peculiar warmth in his heart. He began to care about this peaceful man, Jesus.

He saw the soldiers throw dice to gamble on Jesus' blood-stained robe.

He heard the soldiers mocking Jesus.

"If Jesus is crazy, why not just ignore Him? If Jesus has no followers, why not just let Him go? If they have nothing to fear, why kill Him? They would kill a king if he had a kingdom," he thought to himself.

At the same time, the criminal on the other side of Jesus also observed Jesus.

Both criminals saw the same Jesus. Both criminals heard the same words from Jesus.

But, unlike the penitent criminal, the other criminal saw Jesus from a different perspective.

The other criminal saw Jesus through the lens of cynicism.

"So, you are the Messiah. Are you? Then prove it by saving yourself and us," he shouted at Jesus.

"Don't you fear God?" the penitent criminal asked the cynic.

That remark surprised the people around the cross.

Only a few minutes before, the same criminal who rebuked the cynic had cursed Jesus. Now he was defending Jesus. Everyone looked at him. No one could believe he would care about anybody.

The people around the cross knew the penitent criminal.

He had always been a bully and a brat.

But now that he was about to die, he performed the noblest act. He spoke on God's behalf. The crowd around the cross did not expect him to do so.

Where were those who were expected to defend Jesus?

Peter and the other disciples had abandoned Him.

Jesus' countrymen demanded Jesus' death.

"Don't you ever fear God? We deserve to die for our deeds. But this Jesus has done nothing wrong," the penitent criminal told the cynic.

While he was still alive and hanging on the cross, the penitent criminal turned to Jesus as his only last hope and said, "Remember me when you come into your kingdom" (Luke 24:42).

He did not make excuses. He just desperately asked for help.

At this point, Jesus on the cross performed the greatest miracle, greater than the earthquake and darkness that occurred in Jerusalem that Friday afternoon.

While dying on the cross, Jesus performed the miracle of forgiveness.

The dying, bloodstained Savior received a sin-covered criminal with the words ***Today you will be with Me in paradise!***

This is a mystery, isn't it? Two criminals heard the same words and saw the same Savior.

One saw hope and the other responded with cynicism.

Peter and Judas were disciples of the same Jesus. Peter chose life. Judas hanged himself.

Do you remember Cain and Abel? They were raised by the same parents. Abel chose life. Cain chose death.

Do you remember the Booth brothers, Edwin and John Wilkes? Both were raised by the same parents. They had the same career -- acting. Edwin was a famous actor. John Wilkes assassinated Abraham Lincoln.

A few seconds before he died, the penitent criminal was a beggar at the door of a King's palace, hoping the King would give him a few crumbs.

Suddenly he was given the whole loaf of forgiveness.

No matter how far you have walked away from God, your return trip is only one step. God is one step away from you. God's love and mercy follow you all the days of your life.

We could say that the first canonized saint was not a holy man. He was a repentant criminal.

And it was Jesus Himself who canonized him even before he died.

I am always stunned at God's mercy.

CHAPTER 21

Father, show us where we fit in your loving plan

One day, God struck up a conversation with the devil.

"Hi, devil. Do you see that man (pointing to Job)?" That is a holy man. He does not curse me," God told the devil.

"Of course he is. It is because you bless him. Take away his blessings and he will curse you," the devil responded.

As we know, God temporarily removed His blessings from Job.

How did Job respond when God's blessings were taken away from Him?

This is how Job responded when God took His blessings away.

"Naked came I out of my mother's womb, and naked shall I return thither: the Lord gave, and the Lord hath taken away; blessed be the name of the Lord" (Job 1:21).

We need to know that nothing happens to us without God's permission.

When God allows something bad to happen in our lives we want out. We do not always see trials in life as opportunities for growth.

Scripture says, *"And we know that for those who love God, all work together for good, for those who are called according to his purpose"* (Romans 8:28).

"All" means the good and the not-so-good.

Do we really believe that God is working all things toward our good?

If we do, then our greatest challenge is to allow hard, painful, tear-filled experiences to become our teachers in the classroom of life.

This was what St. Joseph, the foster father of Jesus, did.

If we look back on our life, we can see that we developed our character not in easy times. The greatest lessons of life are often the product of heartaches.

And what we learn in our pain helps us ease the pain of others.

In this sense, our pain is not wasted.

We need to know that God does not waste anything.

Everything that happens in our lives, including pain and hardship, happens for a reason.

And part of that reason is for us to grow in faith.

When it comes to faith, St. Joseph is a good example for us to imitate.

When we find ourselves in the dark valleys of life, we need to trust in God's loving purpose.

Whatever the valley, God is our Shepherd and He promises to be with us. In hard times, we need to cling to His promise.

"Even though I walk through the valley of the shadow of death, I fear no evil, for you are with me. Your rod and staff will comfort me" (Psalm 23:4), Scripture says.

This was what St. Joseph did.

Joseph believed that God was in control even when his life seemed out of control.

When we find ourselves in a dark valley in our life's journey, we need to trust in the loving purpose of God, as St. Joseph did.

Joseph walked in faith.

To walk in faith is to go against every element of self-preservation ingrained in us.

To walk in faith is to let go of our survival instinct and to completely trust in God's loving hands.

To walk in faith is like a trapeze flier completely trusting on the trapeze catcher.

It is an instinct in us to want to take charge, to manipulate, and to control the situations in our lives.

Faith, on the other hand, involves trusting in the love of the Father, Who makes no mistakes.

St. Joseph's life was filled with dark, difficult experiences, yet the final outcome was amazing.

With his bedrock faith in God, Joseph became a godly man in an ungodly culture.

We do not know a lot about St. Joseph.

We know that his father's name was Jacob and that he was the husband of Mary.

We know that he was a carpenter, that after he was engaged to Mary, he found out that Mary was pregnant, and that to protect her reputation, he decided to quietly divorce Mary.

Though the Gospel describes Joseph as a righteous man, there is no mention of Joseph saying anything.

We know that Joseph followed the religious law by going to Jerusalem for the Jewish festivals.

We know that Joseph followed the civil law by going to Bethlehem for the census which was ordered by the Roman emperor.

We know that Joseph had dreams and followed what God told him in those dreams.

We know that Joseph was a man of action.

He did what the angel told him and he took Mary as his wife.

He went to Bethlehem. When he could not find any vacancy in the inns, he found a stable for the night.

When King Herod ordered the death of all the baby boys in Bethlehem, he took his family to Egypt. He followed what an angel told him.

Through the centuries, scholars and artists have tried to figure out what Joseph might have said.

Michael Card, an American singer and songwriter, wrote a Christmas song about Joseph. It is one of my favorite Christmas songs.

I love the words Michael Card put in Joseph's mouth.

Did Joseph say them? I doubt it.

Here are the lyrics of the song:

How could it be, this baby in my arms,
Sleeping now so peacefully,
The son of God, the angel said.
How could it be?
Lord, I know He is not my own,
Not my flesh, not my bone.
Still, this baby is the son of my love.
Father, show me where I fit this plan of yours.
How can a man be a father to the Son of God?
Lord, for all my life I have been a simple carpenter.
How can I raise a king? (Printed with permission).

What a model Joseph is to us. He is a man of God's will. He longed to see God's will. He searched to see how he fit into the Father's plan.

And just as God had a plan for Joseph, God has a plan for each of us.

Unlike Joseph, we may not know God's plan for our life through dreams.

But God orchestrates events and situations to accomplish His plan for each one of us.

There is no event or person that God would not use to accomplish his plan for our lives.

Like Joseph, we may not see the fruit of our labor. We may never reap the harvest. This was true for many heroes of the Scriptures.

It was promised to David that his line would continue forever, but David did not live long enough to see the promise fulfilled.

Abraham did God's will. God promised to give him land. Abraham never saw the fulfillment of God's promise to him, but the promise was fulfilled.

Joseph may have been a simple carpenter, but he is one of the greatest saints in the Church.

In 1870, he was declared the patron saint of the Universal Church.

Let us allow St. Joseph to guide us and to open our hearts to God's plan so that we may become like him –upright and righteous; that we may become a person after God's will; that we may be able to pray, "Father, show me how I fit into this plan of yours."

Author's Biography

"Leandro (Lany) Maniwang Tapay, a native of Balilihan, Bohol, Philippines. His pursuit of knowledge earned him a Bachelor's Degree in Education with a major in English and Spanish, along with a minor in Social Sciences. Continued his theological studies abroad and expanded his expertise by earning a Master's Degree in Guidance and Counseling at the Ohio State University in Columbus, Ohio, USA. His educational journey reflects a diverse and extensive commitment to learning across various disciplines and geographical locations..

Lany's professional journey extends beyond traditional teaching roles, encompassing a diverse range of responsibilities. He began by imparting knowledge of Religious courses at Cebu Boys' Town in Cebu City, Philippines, fostering spiritual growth among students. Transitioning to the United States, he undertook the position of teaching Latin and Religion Courses at Saint Mary High School in North Dakota, where he also served as the Dean of Boys at Saint Mary's boarding school.

His commitment to holistic education extended to Central Catholic School in Toledo, Ohio, USA, where he taught Christian Meditation courses, emphasizing the importance of contemplative practices. His dedication to education and guidance reached new heights as the Guidance Director at London High School in London, Ohio, demonstrating his proficiency in counseling and support for students.

In a testament to his dedication to education accessibility, Lany engaged in moonlighting as he taught Philosophy Courses at Urbana University's outreach program at the London Prison Facility, showcasing a commitment to extending education to diverse settings.

Additionally, Leandro took on the significant role of Diocesan Director of the Pontifical Mission Societies in the United States, Diocese of Columbus, demonstrating leadership in fostering mission-driven initiatives within the diocese.

Beyond his professional endeavors, Lany displayed a compassionate side as a 24/7 caregiver, showcasing his selfless commitment to the well-being of others. Through this multifaceted journey, Leandro has left an indelible mark not only as an educator but also as a caregiver and community leader."